CULTURE OR ART?

Oliver V. Brennan

CULTURES APART?

The Catholic Church and
Contemporary Irish Youth

VERITAS

Published 2001 by
Veritas Publications
7/8 Lower Abbey Street
Dublin 1

ISBN 1 85390 535 6

British Library Cataloguing
in Publication Data.
A catalogue record for
this book is available
from the British Library.

Cover design by Bill Bolger
Printed in the Republic of Ireland by Betaprint Ltd, Dublin

Veritas books are printed on paper made from the wood pulp of
managed forests. For every tree felled, at least one tree is planted,
thereby renewing natural resources.

Dedicated to the memory of my parents,
Patrick and Catherine,
who embraced change
with wisdom and courage.

CONTENTS

INTRODUCTION

This book examines the paradigmatic change that is occurring with regard to young people's affiliation to the Catholic Church in Ireland, particularly as this is reflected in their withdrawal from participation in the weekly celebration of the Eucharist. A significant social and cultural shift has occurred in Ireland during recent decades, on the heels of very rapid economic expansion, paralleling that which occurs in advanced industrial and technological societies generally. In examining the impact of socio-cultural change on the beliefs, values, attitudes and behaviour of young people, the unique Irish situation is explored in the light of contemporary Western culture, which appears to be characterised by a fading modernity and a rising post-modernity.

The research design that is employed to explore the faith-culture nexus combines theoretical, quantitative and qualitative methodology. The findings of the study that led to the writing of this book demonstrate that contemporary Western youth culture, which is characterised by relativism, undifferentiated pluralism, and a deep suspicion of institutions, adversely affects the possibility of young people's commitment to religious institutions. On the other hand, there is clear evidence among the young of a new openness to the mystical and spiritual dimension of human experience, as well as a new search for community. This penchant for the spiritual and for new forms of community augur well for a community-based religious faith such as that embodied in the Catholic Church. Much, however, will depend on the type of community experience that is offered.

Chapter I allows the voices of five different categories of young Irish people to be heard as they tell their life stories, beginning in early childhood. Chapters II, III and IV set out to shed some light on what most influences the beliefs, values, attitudes, and behaviour of young adults in Ireland, with particular reference to the reasons why they are rapidly abandoning Church affiliation. This is pursued in the context of the wider Western world. Having come to a better understanding of what most influences the structure of young people's human and religious experience, chapter V examines the contribution that significant religious educators have made in the area of faith and culture. Finally, chapter VI explores a religious education and pastoral response to the unprecedented situation facing the Catholic Church in Ireland at the beginning of the third millennium of Christianity. It also outlines a set of principles that should underpin a post-modern educational and pastoral response to this new reality. Since the Church/culture relationship in Ireland has evolved to mirror that throughout Western civilization, both the sources used and the conclusions drawn are pertinent to this problem throughout the Western world.

The successful inculturation of the gospel message into the Irish cultural landscape will require much energy and enthusiasm on behalf of Church leaders, religious educators, youth ministers and pastoral care agencies. It devolves upon Church leaders to produce a viable strategic plan that will form the basis of a new pastoral and educational strategy to deal with the issue of faith and culture among the rising generation.

CHAPTER I

THE VOICES OF CONTEMPORARY IRISH YOUTH

One of the best ways to understand a system or a process is through listening to the experiences of the individuals involved.[1] The following five stories serve to illustrate the relationship of contemporary Irish youth to institutionalized religious faith as embodied in the Catholic Church and point to the dramatic changes that have occurred in recent years. These stories are based on transcripts from a series of in-depth interviews with each young person and careful attention has been given to ensure that they are a precise reflection of the dialogical exchange that occurred.

Brigid's Story

I was born in a small town in Northern Ireland. My parents were both from the South, but they moved to Northern Ireland just before we were born. I remember the early years at home being very good and I have a lot of very nice memories about my childhood. I have one older sister and two younger sisters. Although we were Catholic, some of our best friends as children were Protestants. This was quite unusual and was probably due to the fact that Mam and Dad were not from the North.

My parents were fairly religious but we did not pray as a family, at least not in the sense of saying the Rosary every night. At special times we had family prayer. Around the time of my First Communion, I went through a very religious phase and even wanted to be a nun. All this was probably due to the influence of the Primary Three teacher, as she was a very nice person and very religious. It was a convent primary school and we had a lot of fantastic nuns there who put great emphasis on religion.

Throughout primary and secondary school we went to Mass together as a family every Sunday; that went without saying. Going to

Mass with my family each Sunday, as well as to other religious events, gave me a sense of belonging to the parish community. There was a sense of camaraderie about all of that.

At the age of twelve, when I was just beginning my second year at post-primary school, my family moved from the small town where I spent my childhood to a totally rural area. In this parish there was a very strong sense of community and I quickly became involved in various activities, especially a traditional Irish folk group and also the church choir who used modern, appealing hymns and music. The folk group was run by a priest who was in residence in the parish. He worked for the diocese but was very involved with the youth of our area. We travelled a lot to various concert halls and had great fun. I really enjoyed that and it has become a great memory of my adolescent years. At a more explicitly religious level, I used to read at Mass and that same priest would involve us in folk Masses and in the choir for Christmas and other special times of the year. We also sang at a number of radio Masses. All this involvement in the parish kept me interested in religion throughout my time at secondary school.

I had loved primary school and now I really liked secondary school as well. Although this was also a convent school, it did not influence me religiously in the way that primary school did. This was probably due to the fact that religion was no longer interwoven into everything that went on in the school; there were just two religion classes per week. I was also beginning to question some of the tenets of the Catholic religion.

During my years at secondary school, the changing Irish culture did not impinge on me to any great extent. In terms of living in Northern Ireland, you identified strongly with your own religious community and with the people within your school. From that perspective, I would say that I was heavily influenced by my own culture. This, however, was destined to change very soon.

At the age of eighteen I went to college in Dublin and began a degree in law. I soon realized that the study of law did not appeal very much to me. In fact, the only dimension of law that I liked concerned human rights. This is one of the very few elements of law where people are looking for justice rather than just an outcome.

As soon as I moved away from home, I stopped going to Mass, or at least, I would go very, very rarely. There was one church in Dublin that had good music, so I went to Mass there a couple of times. It was a folk Mass and there was a very good priest there. He was very broadminded and I went back to hear him speak a few times. I felt the priest really had something to say and was not just going through the motions. I did not care so much any more for the ritual of Mass. I think there is a lot to be said for ritual in general, for honouring the sacred in things and there is so much of the sacred in everyday life. The ritual of the Mass, however, left me cold.

As I progressed through college, the only link I had with the Church was through attending Mass at the weekends that I spent at home, and this was only to appease my family. There were just two occasions when I really wanted to be there: Christmas and Easter. I enjoyed the ritual of the Christmas Mass because it was very joyful; it was a celebration of birth and of life. The one ritual of the Catholic Church which I think is beautiful, and which I still hold dear, is the Easter Vigil. I think it is very symbolic, as everyone shares the same light. I always thought that was a really special ritual.

During my time at the university in Dublin, my perception of religion became increasingly negative. I was now immersed in a whole new culture that bore little or no similarity to the culture of my childhood and adolescence. I was exposed to different ways of thinking and acting. In addition, I was thrown into a much more pluralistic type of culture than the one in which I grew up. All this invited me to look at some of the beliefs that I had taken for granted and reassess them from the ground up. I began to realize that what is right or wrong depends on the individual. What people do is their business and it is not my place to judge them.

The university chaplaincy never encroached on my life in the slightest and I had a totally secular experience of life during my years of study there. If I had been interested at all, it would have been easy to seek it out, but at that stage I really felt that the Catholic Church was not for me anymore. I would have felt that while there were definitely many things about the Catholic Church that were very valuable, the whole parcel did not appeal to me anymore. Ironically, it was a priest who was responsible for my final break with the Catholic Church. I have an uncle who is a very hard-core or ultra-conservative Catholic priest. He is insistent that one cannot pick and choose what part of the Catholic religion one likes. After much discussion with him, I concluded that I had to reject all of it. I did not want to reject all of it, as there are so many aspects of the Catholic religion that I like, but I felt I had no choice.

Travel has probably been the greatest influence in forming my outlook on life. After I completed my studies at the university in Dublin, I travelled extensively, spending time in Australia, Thailand, Indonesia, Malaysia, the United States and Europe. The more I became exposed to different cultures, different ideas and values, the deeper I went beneath my own surface in order to establish my own personal standards, personal morals and personal beliefs. I found myself dipping into various cultures and religious traditions, taking on board what I felt was good and leaving behind what I considered bad.

When I look back on my life to date, I can see that culture has had the biggest influence on my beliefs and values. Yet, I can also recognize the huge influence that my parents, family members and friends have had on my deepest values. Those who cared for me most have had the greatest influence on me. I am always more inclined to listen to the opinions of those who care for me, even if I don't take them on board.

When I reflect on the various institutions in Irish society, I think that the education system has the greatest credibility. On a sliding scale, I would place the Catholic Church really low. I just think that there is a lot of bigotry and untruth that goes on in the name of the Church. I think that there are people in the Church who are very admirable. There are some fantastic priests, very superior people, for whom I have a lot of time and whose credibility I would never question. However, the Church as a whole has tried to protect itself in a way that has not protected the people of Ireland, especially its children. I think there is no worse crime than to sexually abuse a child, and I blame the Hierarchy of the Church for not protecting the children who were victims of paedophiles. These people needed serious help and needed to be away from children and yet they were allowed to remain in situations where children were exposed to them repeatedly. I believe that there is no excuse for covering up in any institution, least of all the Church.

I think that a lot of the teachings of the Catholic Church are really great. Many of the basic precepts, such as loving one's neighbour, caring for people and for the earth, are really, really great. But the Church goes too far when it gets into the specifics of people's lives, when it condemns people for what they do. For example, I think that the Church has no right to go into the sex lives of married people and into celibacy for priests. I think that people need to be given a lot of leeway in how they live their lives, especially in the sexual area. Anyway, most young people do not observe the Church's teachings on pre-marriage sex anymore.

Love is at the heart of my vision of life; that is what makes my world go around. Everything else is secondary to that. I cannot imagine life without love. I do really like to live a rather simple life, be with people that I love and care for, and spend quality time with these people. I see people all around just trying to acquire more and more and using more and more of the earth's resources, whereas I believe in using less and less. I really try to live in harmony with the planet. Life is all about living in harmony with each other and living in harmony with the earth that we share. My life becomes meaningful through paying really close attention to everything that I do, and I ascertain what is important by looking at how things feel inside, by reflecting on how something affects me spiritually and emotionally.

I believe that there is no absolute right or wrong apart from, perhaps, hurting a child. Sexual abuse is always absolutely wrong. What is absolutely right is less clear because I think that what is right for one individual may be completely different for another individual. There are many things that I consider to be wrong but I certainly would not judge somebody else for thinking otherwise. I also think that no religious body or other group has a right to judge them either. I would not be swayed by what any higher religious or human authority says or teaches. I would really look inside myself and look to other people for their opinions rather than to any religious authority.

Love constitutes happiness for me. I do not think I could be complete without love. Inner peace and knowing that I am on the right path are also very important. I believe in living in a way that is not hurting anybody else, living in a way that is helping other people and not taking away from people or things or animals. Among my friends and the small community of people that I am part of, happiness is primarily about love. However, I think there are many people in our society who believe that they can buy happiness. It is something of the future rather than of the present. I would say that most of my generation of Irish youth put too high a value on material things and I think that if they concentrated more on their spirituality and looked inside more, they would have a better chance of finding happiness.

Many young people today are moving away from the individualism that was characteristic of the era that we seem to be leaving behind, the kind of individualism you see in modern Irish society. That selfish individualism is reflected in people who care only about themselves, having little regard for the community or other people in the society. There is another type of individualism that is good. Because there are less micro-cultures and more macro-cultures today, young people are being exposed to different systems of belief and to different ways of life. This gives a much greater opportunity for people to seek out their own path instead of just conforming to the religion in which they were raised. Individualism is good if it is about searching for your path in life and looking for a route to help others with that. I think young people are becoming less and less likely to project their set of moral values onto other people and this form of individualism is good. More and more young people are looking inside for their answer to what is morally right and that is good; it is certainly much better than just taking a strict set of guidelines from, say, the Catholic Church.

Even though I have moved away from a Church that I consider to be a very non-flexible rigid institution with a rigid set of values, belief in God is still very important to me. The image I have of God is that of a very creative energy, an energy that exists all around us, a life-force. God is always very honest and true and kind and patient. The God that I believe in is very, very good and caring. The notion of a God who sent people to hell never really rang true with me. I believe that all life-forces have a unity and that God is in the connection of all that has life – all human life, animal and plant life, the air, the rivers, the seas, the mountains – God is in absolutely everything around us. When I pray to God it takes the form of giving thanks for everything that is around me; it is an appreciation of the giftedness of life. So while I have grown very cynical or suspicious about institutional religion, my belief in God and my prayer-life are very strong.

Although my personal belief in God and my personal philosophy is not in complete accord with that of the Catholic Church, it is hard to know today how much of my make-up comes from growing up in the Church. I suppose I have been influenced all my life by the Catholic Church, especially in childhood and adolescent years. If I had never been exposed to that Church my values might have been different. While I do not think it influences my values at the moment, there could be an implicit influence there all the time. The deep appreciation I have for ritual may even have come from there.

I intend to pass onto my children many of the beliefs and values that I received from my parents – the centrality of love and sharing, as well as the importance of education. I definitely want to pass on a concept of God to them, even if it will not be quite the concept that my parents gave to me. I want to pass on a spirituality to them and an attitude that will never condemn other people for their ways of life, whether they are homosexuals, unmarried couples or whatever. I want to really educate my children to make up their own minds about what is right or wrong for them.

As I look to the future, my greatest hope is that my partner and I will always love each other, have a happy and healthy family life and raise happy children. My strongest hope for the world is that there would be peace in every corner of the earth, that we would clean up our act ecologically and stop the destruction of the planet. My greatest personal fear is that something might go wrong in my marriage and my one great fear for the world is that we will destroy the delicate eco-system in which we live.

Tara's Story

I was born in a provincial Irish town but at the age of five my family moved to a Dublin suburb, a private residential area comprising twenty-five houses. My family consisted of Mam, Dad, and one older brother. We are a very close family and I had a very happy childhood.

My parents grew up in rural Ireland (my Dad on a farm and my Mam in a small town). They both had a very strong religious commitment because of the way they were brought up and, as a result,

I grew up in a home where religion was very important. We were brought up to believe in everything that our parents believed in, and this was very Catholic. We prayed together as a family every morning and evening. Sunday was the quiet day of the week. We all went to Mass together in the morning and returned home to the typical Sunday dinner. Then either Dad and myself, or Mam, Dad and myself went for a walk up to the woods or down to the beach. My older brother would sometimes come with us, but as he got older he got too 'cool' for this. Of all the Sunday activities, the one that stands out in my memory as most important was morning Mass. This was absolutely central to my parents' lives.

I attended the local convent primary school. There was a strong religious ethos there with the result that what was imparted religiously at home was reinforced in school. I really loved primary school and was very happy there. I loved the head teacher who was a nun and she was really kind to me. I made great friends there and these girls are still my friends today. Although the school had a strong religious atmosphere and religion class lasted for nearly an hour each day, I do not remember much detail about the content of the lessons. However, I do recall such things as preparing for First Communion and Confirmation, taking part in a play based on the religion programme, and exploring the theme of family.

When I was young, apart from the strict Sunday observance, my family was not actively involved in our local parish. What stands out most about parish life during my childhood years was the presence of a particular priest. When he said Mass he was real and he made the Mass real and would talk to the people afterwards. My brother and I really loved him and wanted him at the house all the time. The only active involvement I had in liturgy was at the school Masses where I was often picked to be a reader. I liked that because it gave me a greater interest in what was going on and I felt really part of it.

While I didn't have any sense of belonging to a parish community at primary school age, I did live in a neighbourhood with a very strong sense of community, a factor that is probably not typical of suburban Dublin. The people in that neighbourhood all came from the same background, mainly rural Ireland, and shared the same beliefs and values – that is why my parents made such good friends with them.

For example, every Sunday morning, at 11.30 a.m., there was a mass exodus from our neighbourhood to the church.

I attended secondary school between the ages of twelve and seventeen, and this school was run by the same order of nuns as my primary school. However, the religious atmosphere there was less intense. This diminished altogether when the nun-principal retired and a lay person took over. We still had religion class three or four times a week but the new principal concentrated more on the academic and on the successful running of the school. As an adolescent I wasn't very interested in having prayers said over the intercom and was very happy with the changed atmosphere. I didn't have any interest in religion class until my last two years at secondary school. My interest here grew when the teacher took up issues that were topical and interesting. We were involved in the discussion and value was put on what we had to say. Similar to my primary school experience, my years at secondary school were very happy, not least because my closest friends were with me.

Life at home during my childhood and adolescent years was very sheltered. I was not allowed out to discos, although nearly everybody else in the school was going out at weekends. I was very lucky, however, because my closest friends were not allowed out either. This made my rather confined existence a lot easier, even though I had some conflict with my parents over this issue. At the same time, my adolescent years at home were very happy. Now that I am in my early twenties, I believe my parents were right in not allowing me out and that is what has made me into the person I am today. I was given the chance to develop my own personality, my own ideals and values, without getting ahead of myself too quickly.

During my first few years at secondary school, my relationship with the parish was more or less as it had been when I was at primary school. Then, when I was about sixteen, I began to go to Mass with my friends, instead of my parents. I clearly remember the first Sunday we didn't go to Mass. We went to a friend's house instead and I thought to myself: 'Oh my God, my parents are going to kill me if they ever find out'! We would go into the back of the church and grab a Mass leaflet so that we would know what the readings were about if questioned when we went home. At no time was I ever invited to take any active part in parish life. The priest whom I admired so much left the parish when I was about thirteen, so Church life hardly influenced me at all during my teenage years.

When I was an adolescent, peer influence was confined to my small group of friends who lived in the neighbourhood. At school, other girls told us about being out to discos and pubs at the weekend. But this didn't really affect us as my friends and I lived in a different world; looking back on it now, we didn't have a clue. It was only after I had left school that peer influence began to affect me fairly significantly. Looking back on my adolescent years, I can see that the strongest influence on my life emanated from my parents. I admit that this was unusual as most of the girls in school were heavily influenced by what went on in the world around them, for example, television, videos, music, fashion, alcohol, drugs. They had much more freedom than my friends and I had and, as a result, we didn't have much contact with them outside of school.

I completed secondary education at the age of seventeen and was offered a place at nursing school in one of the largest hospitals in Ireland. This meant leaving home and living in the heart of Dublin city – a total culture shock. It was also frightening, at seventeen, to be wearing a nurse's uniform and looking after very sick people. Then I came to love my training and really enjoyed nursing. I made very good friends and had a great time. It was my first time living away from home and I began to experience life in a new and liberated way. We were in the pub every night of the week and, although I wasn't taking alcohol (which nobody could believe!), I was totally delighted to be out in a pub, meeting new people and experiencing what I hadn't experienced in my life up to now. We would go out most nights, stay out until all hours, have about two hours sleep, and go into work or class the next day. We had such an exciting and fabulous time. When I moved away from home my values and opinions changed because I was exposed to a different type of culture. During this period, I gradually drifted away from the Church and attendance at Mass became less and less frequent.

Between the ages of eighteen and twenty I had lots of short-term relationships with boys, just having a fling. Then after about two years in nursing school, I entered into a steady relationship with a boyfriend. It was very pleasant for the first couple of years and, then, it suddenly ended a short time ago. We were going out together for a year before our relationship became sexually intimate, and eventually we lived together – much to the disappointment of my parents. I was always taught at home not to do this before marriage. The teaching of the Catholic Church also says that it is wrong. But it is ludicrous to think that young people generally don't have intimate sexual relations before they are married. I am totally against the idea of meeting someone and just going off to sleep with him on the first night. Some of my age group, however, do this. I was a year into the steady relationship before anything sexually intimate happened. Anyway, this relationship came to a sudden end when I discovered that my boyfriend had gone off for a weekend with an eighteen-year-old girl. Luckily enough, I had kept very close contact with the friends I had from my earliest years and also with the friends I had made at nursing school. I knew that they would always be there for me and they were. They were a great support. I had also maintained a great relationship with my parents. They have always been there for me, too. I tell them everything about my life. My friends can't believe it. Even though I don't have the attachment to the Church that they have and even though I don't observe the Church teachings that they observe, their overall values have a big influence on me.

Looking back over my life up to this point, I can see that the key influences on my beliefs and values came from my parents, my older brother, my close friends and just the whole culture of Dublin where there is so much freedom and everybody is out to have a good time. Travel has also opened up a new world to me. Over the next six months I intend to travel much of the world. I intend to see more of the US, then go to Australia, back to the US and then on to Europe before entering graduate school. I think it is so important to enjoy life, to travel, to experience different things, meet different people, and just experience life in a different way.

My years in Dublin city influenced me for the better because I became more open-minded, more willing to experience new things, see different points of view, and take more on board than I could have done three or four years ago. I want to experience life to the full before getting married in the distant future. The culture I experienced at nursing school and in Dublin city generally was so different from that of my childhood and adolescence. This is the new culture in Ireland today and it is brilliant.

Some people say there is a clash of values in Irish society today. Maybe this is true for my parents' generation, but we don't experience this. As I reflect back on my life-story, I can see that my parents have had the biggest influence on my life and they continue to have a significant influence on what I believe to be important. That is not to say that I accept all their values. My generation selects the values that make sense to us and ignores the others. But I know that my overall outlook on life is indebted almost entirely to my parents: the importance of a close family life, including the extended family; caring deeply for other people; being generous and kind and not worrying too much about money. I also believe that there is a strong connection between care and influence. The people who have influenced me so far in life are those who have shown me the most care.

The Catholic Church would have had a big influence on me as a child and, to some extent, as an adolescent. Indeed, some of its teachings continue to influence me. I agree with its teaching on divorce and on abortion. I believe that marriage should be for life – that's a good teaching. Right now, I would see myself as having a loose affiliation with the Catholic Church. Being a Catholic is important to me, but it is somewhat peripheral to my life at present. I have my own beliefs and my own faith and I am quite happy with that. I don't think that I have to be an active member of a parish or go to Mass every week or be involved in various kinds of groups in order to be a good Catholic. We were never involved in the parish when I was growing up. I have nothing against the Catholic Church, although I do not agree with some of its rules and regulations.

In Ireland, during the past number of years, the Church has been getting a severe bashing from the media. This has revolved around the revelations concerning child sex abuse by clergy and religious. I think the media has been very biased and unfair to the Church. The whole media hype in this area reveals how much it is out of touch with how most people see things, especially my generation (all my friends see it the way I do) and, even, my parents' generation. The Church as a whole has not lost any credibility in my eyes because of these so-called scandals. You judge all these people as individuals and it was the individual who performed these hideous acts.

Life is very meaningful for me. I love my career. I have the opportunity to travel extensively. I am very happy and look forward to a future full of happiness. I have a strong belief in God with whom I can relate personally. What I value most in life are my family, my friends and my extended family because I know they will always be there for me. I also prize my faith in a benevolent God – the God of my parents. God is always there too. I imagine God like a bearded fatherly figure, someone who is kind and loving. I suppose that is the image I've had since I was a child. In fact, I can't understand people who don't believe in God. It is just part of me. I pray to God most days – in a conversational kind of way. I pray when I am worried about something and also to say thanks for my family and friends and my happy life. The Eucharist does not have any particular meaning for me, although when I go to Mass I feel better afterwards. The reason why I don't go at present is basically an attitude of indifference. I don't feel any obligation to go to Mass unless I feel like going. I don't see any connection between Mass and everyday living; maybe for my parents' generation there is, but not for me. As far as I can remember, this was never taught to me at school. In fact, whatever religious education I received at school doesn't really influence me now at all. Whatever beliefs and values I have right now came from home. I, in my turn, would like to pass onto my children the core values that I received from my parents.

I do not think there are any absolute truths, any absolute right or wrong. It depends on each person – whatever is true for them. What I believe in is true for me but somebody else might think it is not true for them. It all depends on the individual. I believe in something if it feels right and if it makes sense to me. My friends feel the same way. For example, I believe strongly in some of the Catholic Church's teachings, such as respect for life and family values. There are other teachings regarding artificial contraception and pre-marital sex that I don't believe in. I don't think any of my generation believes in this either. It is up to each person to decide what is right and what is wrong. I suppose it depends on the type of culture you are exposed to. My parents were brought up in a culture where authority was respected, especially the authority of the Church. My generation has been freed from all that. We make decisions based on our own life experience.

I don't think the Church is open enough to the views of young people. We are the generation of today and we are the future generation of the Church. I don't think the Church is open to our opinions or to what young people want from the Church. We experience the Church as being too rigid and authoritarian. If you don't do everything the Church tells you, then you are not regarded as a good Catholic. I don't think we should be told what to do.

Things have changed dramatically in Ireland from the time my parents were young. The Church has not moved at all and things are only going to get worse. The Church should listen more to what young people want and to what life is throwing at them. I just don't think they are open to it at all. If the Catholic Church doesn't move with the rapid changes that are occurring in Ireland at present, it is going to lose more and more people, especially my generation. Nearly all of my age group think like I do in this regard. I have great faith in God, and I don't think that will ever change, but I have no involvement with the Church at present. My friends are very much the same. We have strong beliefs as a result of our upbringing but we don't bother too much with institutional religion. Young people just want to lead the lives they are leading now, having a good time and not being restricted in any way.

As I look to the future, my plan is to go to graduate school and become a nursing tutor. This will enable me to influence the type of training that future nurses receive. I have strong feelings about this. I hope to eventually meet someone with whom I can have the kind of relationship that Mam and Dad have. Then I would like to marry and have children. I hope that the conflict and violence in Northern Ireland will be resolved, that the gap between the rich and the poor in our country can be narrowed, that poverty in the Third World will diminish and that people there will eventually enjoy the good life that we experience here in the Western world. My greatest personal fear is that something would happen to my immediate family or, indeed, my extended family and friends. The next greatest personal fear is that I would have an unhappy marriage. My greatest fear for our world is that things will become worse than they are, that people will stop caring and stop worrying about other people and just basically lead self-centered lives.

When I reflect on life and compare the kind of culture my parents grew up in and the Irish culture that my generation experiences, it is easy to see that whatever type of culture you are exposed to has a big impact on your beliefs and values. The older generation needs to be more open-minded about the younger generation's attitudes and values and come to terms with them, if not actually accept them. Finally, if the Catholic Church wants our generation or our children to be committed members, its leaders will really have to start listening to us with an attitude of open-mindedness and a willingness to change.

Sean's story

I grew up in a small rural parish about four miles from a fairly large provincial town. I attended the local parish primary school from the age of four to twelve and then went to the Christian Brothers secondary school in the nearby town.

My childhood and adolescent years were spent in a very committed Catholic family. We went to Mass every Sunday and every First Friday, as well as to Rosary and Devotions on Sunday evenings. We did not pray much as a family at home. Most of our praying happened in church. I also served Mass from First Class in primary school until the end of second year in post-primary school.

My father died at a young age. I was only nine at the time. This had the positive effect of bonding the family more closely together and also deepened the family's religious commitment. My mother had to take over the dual parenting role and she has had a huge influence on my life, especially in regard to my religious commitment and general values.

There was a very strong community sense in our parish. One of the things I will always remember from the time of my father's death was the extraordinary support that my family received from the parish community. I felt really cared for; everybody was there to help you. While our parish was probably above average community-wise, I would say that rural Ireland was generally like that during my childhood years.

My father had been very involved in the Gaelic Athletic Association at both local and regional level, and I also became very involved with the local football team. It formed a big part of my life during my years at secondary school and afterwards. This helped me to get to know a wider circle of people and, in our area, you could just pop in and out of people's houses at will; the door was always open and there was always a great welcome.

I had a very good experience of primary and secondary school. Religion was taught most days at primary level but only two or three times per week in the Christian Brothers School. I do not remember very much about it. I got on very well with the three or four Christian Brothers who taught me at secondary school and I perceived them as teachers rather than as any kind of religious messengers.

During my early and middle teenage years, my mother still had the greatest influence on my life. However, I was also very influenced by an uncle who really looked after me and from whom I have learned a lot. At this time in my life, I was much more influenced by the culture of the parish than I was by the wider culture that was communicated through the media.

As I progressed through secondary school, I noticed that the teenagers from the urban areas had a totally different background and a totally different outlook on life than we had. This was evident in the clothes they wore and the music they played. They were exposed to a whole different kind of culture than we were. In the culture of my local community, authority was respected, religion was valued and people had a strong sense of community.

After completing the Leaving Certificate, I was not sure what I wanted to do in life, so I went back to school and enrolled in a pre-employment class. That led me into my first job at the age of eighteen. The work entailed travelling throughout Ireland on behalf of the company who employed me. I loved this job very much and it was also a great experience. During this time, I continued to live at home and be involved in my local community. My thoughts and feelings about it never changed and I still tried to be as active there as possible. I went to Mass every Sunday and still went to devotions occasionally. The only thing that disappointed me about the parish was that nobody invited me to take any responsibility at a specifically religious level.

During the years I spent at secondary school, my social life was rather quiet. Unlike the boys from the town, I never took alcohol and did not even go to discos. My social life centered around family and friends and the local community. In contrast, the boys and girls from the town were drinking and going out to discos from about thirteen or fourteen years of age. The rapidly changing Irish culture had hardly touched my life at all. It seems to me that the culture to which a person is exposed determines everything.

I now live in a city and work in the financial field, having recently completed a university degree. I can see that I am now somewhat influenced by the urban culture in which I am immersed. However, I still keep in touch with my family and local community and I continue to hold onto the values that I inherited in my childhood and adolescent years. In contrast, most of my contemporaries are heavily influenced by the rapidly changing Irish culture and do not share many of my values.

The people who have influenced me most in my life are my mother and my family circle. They are the people who have had the biggest impact on me. Some of the teachers I have had in primary and secondary school also influenced me to some extent. There were a number of teachers with whom I got on very well at secondary level and they were always there to help me. With my mother's leadership I was able to guide myself along the 'straight and narrow'; she has played a huge, indirect role in the formation of my current beliefs and values. Looking back on life so far, I can say that those who have cared for me most have had the biggest influence on me.

In secondary school, there were never any classes or discussions on what influences young people's beliefs, values and general attitudes to life. We were not taught anything about how individuals are formed or how society is formed. There was not even a hint about analysing cultural change. We were just taught the ordinary subjects and a bit of religion. Moreover, any little emphasis that was given to the social dimension of the Christian message occurred at primary level.

I have a lot of respect for many institutions in Irish society today, for example, the Catholic Church, the GAA, the education system and the government (especially local government). It is hard to rank these

institutions in order of merit because each of them has had a lot of
influence on me and I would always have had a strong interest in
them. I have always been committed to the Church from an early age
and, hopefully, this will continue. I have a strong family background
in the GAA and I will always have a strong interest in it. The education
system has been good to me and I have much more respect for local
government than most people my age.

In contrast to many people of my age-group and especially those
who are younger, I would agree with most of the teachings of the
Catholic Church. At the same time, I would have to say that the
Church is not adapting very well to the new situation in Ireland. It is
not willing to move with the people. It is still a bit closed to the
cultural changes that are occurring, but it is definitely making
progress. It is moving in the right direction, but needs to pick up
speed. I voted against divorce in the last referendum and I thought the
Catholic Church did a fairly good job through the balanced approach
it took leading up to the referendum. In this case, I think it could have
been a bit more challenging to those who wanted divorce.

When I was growing up, priests and bishops did not listen. People
looked up to them and did not challenge the Church. Even though they
are more open at present, they still have quite a way to go; they need to
leave themselves more open so that people can come to them and have
their views listened to. For example, even though I agree with the Church's
stance on pre-marital sex, I can understand the point of view of young
people who do not agree with it and who do not follow that teaching. The
same is true for artificial contraception. The Church needs to listen to
people's point of view and be more open and more understanding.

I have never become very immersed in the new culture that has
invaded Ireland. I am probably not typical of the majority of my
generation. For example, I have never once watched MTV. I still hold
onto the same values that I inherited from my family and local
community – commitment to the Church, respect for authority, the
importance of family life, caring for neighbours and friends. Many
people today are going it alone whereas I would be different in that I
would always be looking out for people. Nowadays, selfish
individualism is the order of the day. People are just looking out for
themselves and not caring for others.

What gives most meaning to my life at present centres on my relationship with my family, friends and, especially, my girlfriend. Being successful in my present career is also very important. I have a fairly relaxed approach to life. I just basically let things happen and go along with whatever way life takes me. At the same time, I do live up to certain standards – those that come from my family. Right now, my main priorities in life are my family of origin, my career and the future of my partner and myself.

Young people of my age tend to think that what is right or wrong depends on each person. I would have a certain sympathy for their point of view but I believe that there are certain moral standards to be upheld and that there is an actual right and wrong irrespective of what individual people think. I would not go along with the old idea that 'black is black' and 'white is white', but I do believe in holding onto certain objective standards. While there are some things that I do not agree with, my overall position would be pro-Church.

My image of God is of someone who cares for you and looks after you. He is there for you in times of need. There is something there to help you and, if you believe in it, it will look after you. While I do not pray as much as I used to, prayer is still important to me. When I do pray, I just sit down and reflect and have a conversation with God.

The Catholic Church for me is the place where I belong, a place of authority. It is the place where there is somebody there to help you in times of need. The Church was the focal point of the community where I grew up and I still see it in that light. Because I now live in the city, I do not have the same connection with the Church as I had when I lived in rural Ireland. Nevertheless, I still go to Mass every Sunday, no matter how late I am out on a Saturday night.

As I look to the future, my greatest personal hope is that I will have a happy marriage, have a family and raise them in the way that I was raised myself. My greatest hope for the world is that we can all get on well together – rich and poor, East and West. My biggest personal fear is that of failure, especially that my family might not live up to the expectations that I have for them. I would also fear that my immediate family might need something that I could not provide. My one fear for the world is that people might not have a genuine respect for each other or be able to live in harmony.

Fiona's story

I grew up on a farm, the youngest of four children, in what you might call a traditional Catholic family. It was a rather quiet household and my parents were the type of people who were not able to express emotions or feelings very well. My mother, in particular, was a perfectionist and I always felt that I had to prove myself to her. However, no matter what I did, it was never good enough. I did not grow up as a happy child as I was always looking for acceptance and looking for love, but never really experienced it. Luckily, the farm afforded me the possibility of an outdoor life and it was there, in the heart of nature, that I found some happiness and could give free reign to my imagination.

I went to the local primary school at the age of four but, unfortunately, did not find much happiness there either. I was quiet and rather bright, so I became the subject of envy by the other girls in the class. I did not feel accepted and this served to make me even more withdrawn.

My only experience of parish life during primary school centered on attendance at weekly Mass and other religious occasions, thereby being part of a large group of people. My family were not very outgoing, so these were the only times I would have met other members of the parish. Furthermore, there were no parish-based programmes for children or young people.

Regarding my religious experience at home, the clearest memory I have is that of saying the rosary. My dad always led it and it was rattled off as if he was selling cattle. He knew it so well and the words just rang out in a mantra style. I also remember Dad kneeling beside my bed when I was very young and saying night prayers. Religion was just part of life in my home; it was woven into the daily and weekly routine on the family farm. There was also a history of clergy in the family, a tradition of which it was very proud.

Having completed primary school education, I then attended the convent secondary school in a nearby town. This allowed me to move a little more out into the world. However, since I was not a very outgoing person, my main sphere of influence was still the home. My adolescent years were the most depressing, uncertain and insecure years of my life so far, especially the latter years at secondary school, when I was trying to become my own person. What contributed most to my unhappiness was a lack of self-esteem, self-belief, not knowing who I really was, and not being able to accept myself as a person. I had a sense of guilt about everything, a sense that everything I did was wrong, since nothing I ever did was good enough for my mother. I even felt that everything I ever did hurt her in some way. All of this was reinforced by the fact that every time I went to Mass I heard that I had sinned. One of my abiding memories of the Church as an adolescent is that 'you are a sinner and, therefore, you are a bad person'.

During my childhood and adolescent years, I was always struck by the wonder and beauty in nature all around me, for example, a magnificent sunset, but I never found that in the people I encountered or indeed in myself. More recently, I have come to see people as those who are ruining the beauty of our world.

One of the positive experiences of secondary school was the growing realization that I was very intelligent and that I was good at art. This helped to improve my self-esteem. It also gave me the confidence to apply for a degree course at a university. I took up the study of theology and loved it. This was a wonderful, intellectual challenge, even though it did not give me any spiritual satisfaction.

The practice of religion that I observed at home did not change very much in my earlier years at college. I was very good at attending Mass, not only on Sundays, but also on many weekdays, a factor that was probably influenced by my friends – they all studied theology and were very much into attending Mass. Eventually, I began to experience Mass as boring and dead and, consequently, attended less frequently.

After completing the degree in theology, I embarked on a post-graduate course in a secular area. During this period, I felt the need to work on my own spirituality as I was no longer connected to anything religious in the academic field. I gave a significant amount of time to prayer and reflection, making much use of the New Testament. Ironically, the more I became spiritually alive, the less I appreciated the Mass. Gradually, I became very frustrated and ended up not going every Sunday.

My biggest influence at college came from a member of the college staff who was a priest. He was one of the lecturers and he took time to listen to my story and provide the space where I felt wanted, accepted and cared for. At last I found somebody who cared enough to listen to me and my story. It was my first real experience of someone giving unselfishly. The many hours I spent in his presence turned into a sort of religious experience because that is what I had seen Jesus as – a person who was willing to give and provide space. This has had an extraordinary healing effect on my life.

I have now completed post-graduate studies and I am spending a year working, in a voluntary capacity, on a residential school retreat team. So far this has been a very good experience. It is like ministering in a church within a church, where there is great freedom to express yourself in many ways, including prayer and liturgy. My childhood and adolescent experience of rural community is a strong, but fading, memory.

Right now, I believe in the goodness of people and in the presence of Jesus in my life and in other people's lives. I believe in my call to follow him and do as he did: to accept everyone as they are and where they are. I have reached this stage through a lot of personal reflection as well as reflection on scripture, the latter being aided through the formal study of theology. However, none of this might have been possible without the help of the caring priest I met at college, who freed me from much of what enslaved me personally and affirmed my goodness. When you receive care from someone, that person touches you, challenges you and influences your beliefs, values and general outlook on life.

Looking back, I do not think that I got much help from formal religious education or formation. What I now have has come from my own personal development and through the help of a very few people. I think that modern society in general is a society of people that are alienated. Young people of my age are searching to belong somewhere; many of them are very empty and are in great need of care and love. Contemporary culture tells us that we can buy happiness, but this is shallow and empty. It does numb the pain temporarily, but deep down the pain remains.

People of my generation need someone there for them. They are not finding this in the culture and not even in the institutional Church in which they grew up. The Catholic Church, like many institutions in Ireland, is irrelevant to them. It is as if young people are having one conversation and the Church is having another conversation and neither is talking to the other. It is like two people having dinner together who are having totally different conversations as they talk to one another. Young people are living on one level and the Church is on another level without connecting at all.

I am a young person of faith, but I have very lax views on the teachings of the Catholic Church. I probably do not know half of them and I do not think it affects my life or spirituality very much one way or the other. I believe the teachings are not the most important things. One does need a certain amount of teaching because one needs some sort of boundaries or limits, but I think the Church has far too many rules and regulations. The Church's teaching is reminiscent of that of the Pharisees versus Jesus. It does not allow for human experience to be lived and the teachings do not allow for the opportunity to touch human experience. I believe that the Church is a structure that has potential if it could only move away from all the rules and regulations to a more life-filled experience of the truth and of spirit. The Word of God was never meant to grow into old age as the Church has done. I do need Eucharist, even if I experience it as painfully boring and frustrating. Eucharist is very important to me and I think it is the essence of Christian faith. I also desperately need community, but not the traditional authoritarian, hierarchical community where there is no sharing and no input from young people. I believe that there is potential for both a liturgy that is relevant and for a community of shared faith and experience.

What gives most meaning to my life at present is to be there for other people, to be a presence or to be the human face of God for people and to be able to live out of an experience of being loved. I think that faith or spirituality or the truth as Jesus proclaimed it is something that is lived and experienced, and that it is going to be a very subjective or very individual experience. I do not think that anybody can ever grow or mature spiritually unless they experience and experiment with life and one cannot do that if there are any absolutes. Authority for me is the wisdom of the people who have gone before me, but that is not an absolute authority because situations change, people change and culture changes. In order for something to be right or moral, it has to be right in relation to the people around me and not do any damage to, what I consider, the balance or the cycle of life in general.

As I look to the future, my personal hope is that I can continue to be critically committed to the Church. I have a vision of a Church that will offer a place where many people will find belonging and will find truth and hope and love. If given a chance, I can help bring that about. My fear is that my commitment to the Church would chain me down, that the freedom and the spirit that I hold would be chained down and destroyed in rules and regulations. While I have a strong desire to be an active member of the Church, it is hard to be a woman in the Catholic faith community.

My greatest hope for the world is that we would realize the value of people above things, that we would treasure the earth and protect both. Conversely, my greatest fear is that human beings would destroy their own planet and in the process destroy themselves.

Tom's story
I grew up in a local authority housing estate in a socially deprived area of a large Irish town. I was one of three male siblings. My father was one of the few men in the area who had a job and my mother was at home. We were a reasonably happy family and my father and mother got on well, apart from the occasional row.

One of the outstanding memories of my childhood was my first day at school. I hated it, threw a tantrum and was slapped around the legs by the teacher. From the very beginning, I could not handle being in the school system and I have always had an aversion to it. All my memories of primary school are negative. One of the teachers said to our class that by the age of thirty, four of us would be dead and that a lot of us would end up in the gutter for the rest of our lives. It was not the way to motivate children from a deprived area. As a result, I left primary school feeling stupid and good for nothing.

At the age of twelve I entered one of the secondary schools in the town, a school run by a religious order. I carried the negative attitude towards the education system from primary school into secondary school and had a very turbulent three years there before being advised to leave. I began secondary school in the lowest stream. This was, traditionally, the class of 'messers' and 'headers'. I thought 'this is not for me; I'll just have fun here'. Homework and books were just alien to me and I tried to get through the school day with the least amount of hassle.

After Junior Certificate, I enrolled in a VPTP [Vocational Preparation and Training Programme] course at the vocational school in the town. I was not very interested in this either, but it was good because we got paid, monthly, by the government. Before the end of one year, I was asked to leave because of bad behaviour. However, at this stage I began to realize that there was an academic side to my character and, despite my very negative experience of the education system, I also realized that I had other talents. This realization came about through the work of a youth leader who involved my age group in plays and other activities in the local community centre. I then went back to the secondary school and humbly asked them to take me into fifth and sixth year. They accepted me back and I ended up completing my Leaving Certificate.

Our home wasn't very religious, but weekly Mass was important. All the family went to Mass each Sunday. In fact, I attended Mass until I was eighteen years of age. I always believed in God and, in my mid-teens, I began to formulate who God was. I received help from the Christian Doctrine class during my last two years at the secondary school. We had a female religion teacher who gave a lot of time to discussion and who gave us the opportunity to sort out our beliefs. I got the feeling that it was okay to believe in whatever you believed in and to formulate your own beliefs.

When I look back on parish life during my childhood and adolescent years, the big thing that stands out in my mind was a parish youth trip to Medjugorje. I was sixteen at the time and I went there with an open mind. When I got there I was not very interested in the apparitions, or the rosary beads covered in blood, or anything like that. However, I did climb the mountain and directed the whole experience spiritually into myself. I did have a deep spiritual experience there, one that awakened me to my own spirituality. On returning from Medjugorje, a prayer group was set up. I joined this, but I got turned off very quickly because of the fundamentalist Catholic teaching that was so much part of it. The whole focus was on the devil and sin and I found their spirituality very dark.

The other thing that stands out about parish life during my adolescent years was the presence of a few nuns who came to live in one of our council houses. I became very friendly with one of them and built up a good relationship with her. I was looking for answers and this help me a lot in those years. I did not have much contact with priests, apart from one of the curates who was friendly with my mother and called to our house sometimes. In fact, I had no contact with the parish apart from Sunday Mass. The person who probably influenced me most when I was growing up was a youth leader in the area. He had a very open-minded and liberal way of looking at things and that suited me. I always felt deeply respected by himself and the nun.

Pop culture had a very definite influence on me during my adolescent years: rock music, MTV, bands, films. I was drinking in all that stuff. The music and songs made me very critical of the adult world generally, especially institutions, traditions and authority.

At the age of nineteen I left home and enrolled in a course in Applied Social Studies and Social Care at a regional college. It was around this time that I stopped going to Mass, but I did not pack in the Church completely for another year or so. I did not make a conscious decision to sever any connection I had with the Catholic Church; it just happened. The only Church-related religious experiences that I had at college were a visit to a small Protestant church with a Protestant friend and a visit to a cathedral on my own. The first was a very real ceremony; it was a very small congregation and was very inclusive as each person was allowed to share their little bit of spirituality. The cathedral experience was very nice but different. There was a lovely choir and a brass band playing but I had no part in it; it was like being at a concert.

During my time at college, I read a lot about Eastern religions and I liked the whole train of thought there, especially the unity of body, mind and soul. This also led me to believe that there is more than one way to God and that the Catholic Church does not have a copyright on the whole thing. I now believe in a higher power and I do believe that Jesus Christ was on this earth. Jesus was a very real figure but I think that is lost in the Church's teachings. He had to be proclaiming a powerful message and there had to be something very charismatic about him to get people to 'down tools' and follow him.

Having grown up in the latter end of a Catholic society, it would be unfair to say that I have not been influenced (for the better) by the Church. Without that upbringing, I might not have been able to develop the spirituality I have today, such as it is. I believe very strongly in some of the sayings that I heard or read, such as: 'It is easier for a camel to go through the eye of a needle than for a rich man to enter heaven.' There was probably some emphasis put on the social teaching of Jesus in school and in the church as well, but nothing stands out in my mind. If it were done with real passion, I would definitely remember it. There is no point in reading out the odd circular at Mass on justice issues unless the Church is very pro-active and involved on the ground. While there are some outstanding exceptions, the Church as an institution is very middle class and, therefore, excludes people of my class.

The young people with whom I now work, the so-called underclass (of whom I am one), all feel alienated from the Church and not only from the Church but from all institutions of the State. In fact, the only institution in the country that I have any regard for is the voluntary sector in which I now work. It cares for the socially deprived and they are connected to it. We have no say in the Church or in the political process and, therefore, we cannot feel connected to them. There is nothing to draw me towards the Catholic Church at the present time. I believe that the voluntary sector could be a model for the Church. They are not the people with all the answers but they are working for people and alongside people.

What gives most meaning to my life at present is helping deprived young people develop their fullest potential. I was lucky in that I was one of the few people of my social background who got a third-level education and I want to play my part in bringing about a change in Irish society that will put an end to the political and social alienation of 30 per cent of the population. I just want to be me and in some way give back what I have got out of life. I also like to belong, to be part of something and have the solidarity that comes from being part of a community. Belief in God is also important to me and I do pray to this Divine Presence in a conversational manner. The most important person in my life at the moment is my girlfriend with whom I live. I know Church people think this is immoral, but I love my girlfriend and in my eyes it is right. Even though the Church to me is non-existent, if we have a child, I would want my child baptized as a Catholic for whatever reason.

As I look to the future, my greatest hope is that I do myself justice and do justice to those connected to me. My hope for the world in general is that we would wake up and smell the roses, that we would realize that we are burning the fuse of an ecological time-bomb. How much do we have to own? Where does success end? My greatest personal fear is that, amid all the chaos, we disintegrate and become broken. My fear for our world is that people will become less and less important, especially the poor, and that greed will destroy the whole eco-system.

Understanding a new reality

These five stories paint a vivid picture of the current reality in Ireland regarding the beliefs, values, and Church affiliation of five different categories of Irish youth. Less than three decades ago, Sean's story of Church affiliation would have been that most characteristic of Irish youth, urban or rural. At the beginning of the third millennium of Christianity, the other four stories have come to represent more than half the young population of Ireland and are becoming increasingly characteristic of a new reality. These stories tell of a growing problem for the Catholic Church in Ireland. A paradigmatic shift seems to be occurring with regard to young people's Church affiliation. Tom is representative of the vast majority of socio-economically deprived urban youth who are largely alienated from the Church. Tara represents a significant section of university and tertiary-level students who are disinterested in any form of institutionalized religion. Fiona's story is illustrative of a growing number of reflective young people, especially women. They are searching for a meaningful spirituality, not necessarily, but ideally, lived out in the institution of the Church. Brigid's story mirrors that of a small number who leave the church of their parents and grandparents in order to join other religious groups or sects.

Why is it that young people reared in families characterized by a strong commitment to church are disowning the faith community into which they were nurtured and socialized? Some of the most recent research available in Ireland indicates that university students aged between eighteen and twenty-two, as well as university graduates, have lower than average levels of traditional religious practice.[2] A decline in

Church affiliation corresponds with third-level education, in contrast to the much higher percentage of those with lower levels of education who attend Church weekly. This is ominous for the Catholic Church in Ireland since the number of young people attending universities and third-level institutions of various kinds is increasing dramatically.

The attitude of young Irish men and women towards the Church can be characterized as 'indifference', not enmity.[3] This suggests the influence of post-modernity rather than of modernity. The latter tends to be hostile toward religion and the former, while more spiritually open is, in fact, more apathetic.[4] While there is evidence that a spiritual hunger exists among young people today, they appear to be indifferent toward, and even suspicious of, institutionalized religion. Data suggest that a significant cultural shift has occurred in Ireland on the heels of rapid economic expansion, paralleling that which occurs in advanced industrial societies generally.[5] This is affecting the rising generation more than any other group. Ireland is becoming an increasingly urbanized society and the most recent research shows that the majority of young urban Irish people have turned their backs on a part of Irish life that was almost universal three decades ago.[6] What is even more disconcerting is that less than 7 per cent of young people in the socially deprived urban areas have any real attachment to the Church. In these areas, the weekly celebration of the Eucharist has been virtually abandoned.

In endeavouring to understand this new religious phenomenon in Irish society, it is necessary to explore how economic, social, and especially cultural changes, affect people's beliefs, values, meanings and religious commitment. It is to this that we now turn.

Notes

1. J. E. Seidman, *Interviewing as Qualitative Research: A Guide for Researchers in Education and the Social Sciences* (New York: Teacher's College Press, 1991), p. 3.
2. C. T. Whelan and T. Fahy, 'Religious Change in Ireland 1981–1990', in *Faith and Culture in the Irish Context* ed. E. G. Cassigy (Dublin: Veritas, 1996), pp. 100–116.
3. M. MacGréil, *Prejudice in Ireland Revisited* (St Patrick's College Maynooth: The Survey and Research Unit, Department of Social Studies, 1996).
4. M. P. Gallagher, *Clashing Symbols: An Introduction to Faith and Culture* (London: Darton, Longman & Todd, 1997).
5. R. Inglehart, *Culture Shift in Advanced Industrial Society* (Princeton: Princeton University Press, 1990).
6. A. Hanley, 'Major Religious Confidence Survey', in *Intercom* (Dublin: Veritas, March 1998), pp. 18–19.

Chapter II

Faith and Culture in Western Society

As Western society has become increasingly secularized there has been a corresponding weakening of religious beliefs and practice among many people, especially the young. The work of sociologists and anthropologists points to the fact that people's beliefs, values, and attitudes have influential social origins. Doyle McCarthy points out that in the writings of the French, German, and American sociological traditions, 'the sociology of knowledge argues that society's influence extends into the structure of human experience in the form of ideas, concepts and systems of thought.'[1] She goes on to say that 'social life provides the stuff (words, gestures, attitudes) out of which conscious life develops.'[2] When social and economic changes occur, they usually have the effect of causing significant cultural shifts, although the latter change is slower than the cause. Since culture impacts powerfully on people's lives, it is essential to understand its nature in order to appreciate how it affects religious belief and practice. In particular, as Michael Warren notes, 'the situation of young people cannot be properly understood without attention to how social and cultural forces affect them.'[3]

Toward a Definition of Culture

Culture, as a social phenomenon, has been studied by empirical researchers and theorists in the fields of anthropology, sociology, philosophy, psychology, and religion. Each of these sciences has contributed to both the understanding of culture and the development of its definition, even though each approach has given its own weight and importance to various elements involved in the production, continuation, and evolutionary direction of culture.

For theology, religious education, or pastoral ministry to have a significant influence on culture, its forms and directions, and on the individual's response to one's ambient culture, theologians, religious educators and those in church ministry need to understand the history, conclusions and attitudes of the new sciences, as well as contemporary philosophical understandings and perspectives. In addition, particular emphasis must be given to an appreciation of (a) the mechanism by which each contributing element arises, grows, and exerts its influence, and (b) the motivation of those introducing each element and/or promoting its growth and influence. These two factors are of importance in the determination of whether this particular element is constructive or destructive with regard to the moral and ethical well-being of society.

It is generally agreed that 'the very word "culture" is problematic, with no fixed, agreed-upon definition.'[4] Through an examination of the literature on the topic, certain characteristics do become clear. Current approaches to understanding culture differ significantly from the traditional, classical notion of culture as enunciated by Matthew Arnold more than a century ago. For him, culture was the preserve of the elite, of those who leaned toward the aesthetic and toward excellence, an inward condition that was at variance with the mechanical and material civilization of the industrial age. It was primarily the province of intellectuals and academics. But even in Arnold's time, this notion of culture was being expanded by the British anthropologist Edward Tylor to include 'knowledge, belief, art, morals, law, custom and any other capabilities acquired by [a person] as a member of society.'[5]

In the first half of the twentieth century, Tylor's approach was given a much wider meaning by anthropologists and sociologists. Instead of the strong association of culture with the worlds of thought and art, this concept was becoming synonymous with a way of life. 'Throughout this century, the idea of culture has become not only the province of intellectuals and academics, but a feature of a common world view and an idea used in ordinary speech.'[6] It is now generally accepted that 'culture constitutes a total context that shapes us all.'[7]

Clifford Geertz emphasizes the crucial role of symbols as carriers of culture. In his words:

> Culture denotes an historically transmitted pattern of meanings embodied in symbols, a system of inherited conceptions expressed in symbolic forms by means of which [people]

communicate, perpetuate and develop their knowledge about and attitudes towards life.[8]

This semiotic approach to the study of culture is directed toward what Doyle McCarthy calls 'the study of symbolic and signifying systems through which a social order is communicated and reproduced' and 'these signifying systems and social practices are what make up a culture and its structures of meaning.'[9] In this semiotic concept the human being is, as Geertz puts it, 'an animal suspended in webs of significance he himself has spun.' Those webs of significance constitute culture and the analysis of it is 'not an experimental science in search of law but an interpretive one in search of meaning.'[10] This understanding of culture, which includes the crucial role of symbols as carriers of culture, is of particular significance when one reflects on the dynamic of culture and religious faith.

In considering the impact of culture on religious belief and practice, it is important to note its historical dimension, one of the six categories identified by Kroeber and Kluckhohn.[11] In this regard, Alyward Shorter's definition is helpful: 'Culture is, therefore, essentially a transmitted pattern of meanings embodied in symbols, a pattern capable of development and change, and it belongs to the concept of humanness itself.'[12] It follows that since religion is a human phenomenon, it inevitably affects, and is affected by, culture. Because of the historical dimension, because by its nature culture seeks to pass on its cumulative wisdom from one generation to the next, an inherited culture can be severely challenged during a period of rapid social change. What has occurred in Ireland in recent decades is a good illustration of this phenomenon.

It is clear from this brief outline of the evolution in the understanding of culture that the definition of the concept has changed significantly in the past century, paralleling in its evolution the increasing importance ascribed by sociologists, anthropologists, philosophers, and other scholars to culture as the dominant factor in the internal and external relationships of any society. The findings of critical history put an end to the classicist assumptions that understood culture in a narrow, unitarian manner, a normative view of culture that, according to Shorter 'inhibited the Church's missionary activity' and 'distorted the Church's own understanding of itself.'[13] It is now generally accepted that the manner in which people experience reality, especially the young, is culture-bound. Since culture is a developing process rather than a static entity, and since religious faith can only exist in a cultural form, there needs to be continuous dialogue between Christianity and culture.

Cultural Change and Its Impact on Christian Faith

I share the conviction of Thomas Groome that 'the more adequately we understand the culture of our time and place – and especially its ways of knowing – the more likely we are to be effective religious educators.'[14] To understand the significant cultural change that has occurred in the Western world over the last two centuries, examination is required of the concepts of modernity and post-modernity, which have characterized this period. Before proceeding with this discussion, however, it is important to briefly review the key philosophical and theological elements in pre-modernism.

Pre-modernity

In the pre-modern world people were very attuned to the rhythm of the seasons and of the day. The cycles of nature and the events of history were described through narrative rather than through science or history. Metaphysically, pre-modernity was marked by an adherence to universals and absolutes: a particular truth was always and everywhere true. The world was viewed as complete and fixed for all time and was marked by the harmony of an objective order. It was understood in terms of well-defined essences using abstract, universal concepts. Nature had its own intrinsic form and this was paralleled by intrinsic finalities in human behaviour. Divine revelation ended with the canonical scriptures and the truths of revelation were fixed for all time.

In the culture of pre-modernity, the method of inquiry that was used to interpret both human existence and Christianity was primarily deductive. It began with abstract reality rather than human experience, and principles were derived from universal essences. The conclusions reached had a certain permanence and were always right as long as the deductive logic was correct. V. A. Harvey argues that the basic confrontation underlying the claims and counter-claims of traditional Christianity and the modern sciences centres on morality.[15] In this regard, Richard Gula offers a description of the classicist world-view of moral theology and the moral life. Traditional moral theology abstracted from the concrete to deal with issues in the abstract and universal realm. It 'deals with universals of humanhood by deriving principles from the physical nature of being human' and it 'conforms to authority and to pre-established norms.'[16] Pre-modern morality emphasized duty and obligation in order to reproduce the established order. The source of moral norms was the natural law; they were written in nature. God is the author of nature and, as Gula puts it, 'God-given structures take priority over anything derived from human reflection.'[17] Knowledge of moral norms could be gained by observing the way nature works and any interference with the order designed by God was regarded as gravely serious.

Theology was also deductive in the pre-modern world, in contrast to its largely empirical nature today. Bernard Lonergan says that theology 'was a deductive science in the sense that its theses were conclusions to be proven from the premises provided by Scripture and Tradition.'[18] In response to the rise of modern science and the Enlightenment with its concomitant attack on Christianity, theologians at the end of the seventeenth and early eighteenth centuries introduced 'dogmatic theology'. This term was already in use to denote a distinction from moral, ethical, or historical theology. Its new meaning designated its opposition to scholastic theology. In the words of Lonergan, 'it gave basic and central significance to the certitudes of faith, their presuppositions and their consequences.'[19] He goes on to state that this type of dogmatic theology 'had misconceived history on a classicist model, that it thought not in terms of evolution and development but of universality and permanence.'[20]

David Tracy believes that much traditional Christian self-understanding is in a state of 'cognitive, ethical and existential crises.'[21] As will be seen later in this book, this crisis is reflected in the beliefs, values, and behaviour of contemporary youth. The papal documents that deal with reproductive sexual morality are grounded in a pre-modern world-view and this is the domain in which young people are most distanced from Catholic Church teaching.

Modernity

According to Michael Paul Gallagher, 'modernity stands for a cultural condition, as distinct from modernization which refers to more technical developments such as means of transport or of production.'[22] The two went hand in hand, but 'the end result was a greatly altered context for human belonging and human self-understanding, entailing a gradual but total break with pre-modern ways of life.'[23] The arrival of modernity is best considered in terms of successive waves rather than as one historical moment. These waves have had the cumulative effect of diminishing religious commitment for masses of people.

Modernity is often portrayed as rooted in the Enlightenment and in the political movements embodied in the American and French revolutions. Since Enlightenment and Revolution together represent a certain revolt against institutions and against traditional forms of authority, they were met with much suspicion and resistance by the nineteenth-century Catholic Church. There is clear evidence of this in the case of the French Revolution where the Catholic hierarchy sided with the monarchists.

From a social perspective, the Industrial Revolution brought in its train another 'modernity wave' in that it caused a new cultural consciousness. Doyle McCarthy notes that:

> A long-standing modern motif is the apparent fragmentation of personal identity due to the rise of industrial culture and its weakening of the great stabilizing and integrating forces of human existence (religion, labour, and language), and their replacement by the vast, complex and artificial structures of technical civilization.[24]

This era also witnessed the retreat of faith into a more private realm, as urbanization eroded older forms of community and challenged the traditional and more rural embodiments of religious faith.

The final wave of the cumulative phenomenon of modernity, and the greatest of all, was due to the technological revolution: first the radio, then television, and quickly on its heels, computers and information technology, which is producing the greatest cultural revolution of recent times and, perhaps, of all time. 'We live in a world,' says Doyle McCarthy, 'almost overwhelmed by its own inventiveness, its own artificiality. Our realities exist in transmission – on screens and cables – and our sense is that those who possess and control knowledges and images and sounds effectively control our realities.'[25] Michael Paul Gallagher claims that 'the very rhythms of human consciousness have been altered by this world of fast-moving data and images' and that the culture of modernity has 'altered the cultural conditions of the possibility of 'hearing' from which Christian faith is born.'[26]

Charles Taylor outlines three malaises of modernity. The first concerns the growth of individualism in contemporary culture, formulations of which are the 'permissive society', the 'me generation', or the prevalence of 'narcissism'. He says that 'the sense that lives have been flattened and narrowed, and that this is connected to an abnormal and regrettable self-absorption, has returned in forms specific to contemporary culture.'[27] The second malaise concerns the primacy of instrumental reason, 'the kind of rationality we draw on when we calculate the most economical application of means to a given end,' without also taking into account the moral implications. The institutions and structures of technologically advanced societies weaken moral deliberation and cause both societies and individuals to emphasize instrumental reason in a manner that can be highly destructive. An example of this is the thinning of the ozone layer. The third malaise concerns the loss of freedom, the evolution of a society 'where few will want to participate actively in self-government,' opening up the danger of a new, specifically modern form of despotism. The atomism of the self-absorbed individual militates against participation in different levels of government as well as in voluntary associations.

Taylor acknowledges that these three malaises of modernity are controversial both as to their nature and formulation, while others want to dismiss them out of hand. Modernity has its affirmers as well as its detractors. He believes that the essential nature of these developments in modernity is often misunderstood. As a result, 'the real nature of the moral choices to be made is obscured.' Taylor takes the middle path between the uncritical affirmers and the enemies of modernity. He believes that there is much that is admirable as well as much that is debased in all the developments of modernity. The task is to 'steer these developments towards their greatest promise and avoid the slide into the debased forms.'

What gets lost in the critique of many commentators on modernity is 'the moral force of the ideal of authenticity.' The moral ideal of self-fulfilment or authenticity, which is at the heart of modernity, should not be implicitly discredited because of its debased and deviant forms. Taylor regards authenticity as 'a child of the Romantic period, which was critical of disengaged rationality and of an atomism that did not recognize the ties of community.' What is needed is neither outright condemnation nor uncritical praise for what is a constitutive ideal of modernity, namely, being true to oneself. The response to a degraded and trivialized form of the culture of authenticity, Taylor suggests, is to retrieve a proper understanding of this ideal of self-fulfillment and self-realization, thereby enabling people to be true to their own originality. The alternative to this is a narcissistic self-fulfillment that is a deviant and trivialized form of 'an ethical aspiration, the ideal of authenticity.'

A purely personal understanding of self-fulfilment has a very significant impact on Christian faith. The heart of the understanding of discipleship of Jesus of Nazareth involves life in community. This is a core dimension of Christian faith. In the Judeo-Christian tradition, God's self-communicating revelation was always to a community or to an individual-in-community and it invited a community response. The early Church was particularly conscious of Christian faith lived-in-community, as is evidenced in the Acts of the Apostles and other writings. Because the contemporary culture of authenticity encourages a very personal understanding of self-fulfilment, it is, according to Taylor 'antithetical to any strong commitment to community.' When a person does enter into community association, it tends to be for instrumental reasons. This mentality is a severe challenge to a religious belief system built around community.

Post-modernity
The death of modernity and the birth of post-modernity are sometimes traced to the fall of the Berlin Wall in 1989. This may be true in an ideological sense, but one cannot easily ascribe an exact date

to this cultural shift. While one recognizes that this event symbolized the end of one cultural epoch, contemporary Western culture continues to be characterized by elements of modernity as well as post-modernity.

Most religious educators date the origins of post-modernism/ post-modernity to the early 1960s, particularly as it affects young people. Groome says that 'within Western culture, Generation X – twenty-year-olds to thirty-somethings – are cited as most illustrative of how post-modernism is lived out on the ground.'[28] In any event, there is general agreement that Western culture is passing through a paradigm shift and this cultural movement is generally referred to as post-modernism or post-modernity. Thomas Leuze suggests that since we live in a transitional or developing period, the term 'post-modern', though nebulous, is appropriate 'since that which has not yet happened can only be described by what has happened.'[29]

From a philosophical perspective, post-modernism presents a new challenge to the Catholic Church. In post-modern epistemology (i.e., ways of knowing), truth is a dynamic process that human beings experience. It is contextualized and embodied in particular situations by particular people. For the modern epistemologists, there are absolutes, since truth can exist apart from the knower and the holding of differing viewpoints suggests error. In post-modern thought 'Knowing is something persons do . . . there is no knowledge apart from knowers.'[30]

In other words, the philosophy of modernism depended on a foundational statement for validity, whereas the holistic epistemology of post-modernism discovers its strength in the relationship between beliefs; it lauds diversity. In seeking uniformity of belief, with its attending view of disembodied truth, modern epistemology had a comfortable home in the Catholic Church. Post-modern epistemology, with its affirmation of diversity, presents a new challenge.

One feature of the philosophy of post-modernism that appears to be more favourable to a community-based religious faith is the new 'non-individualist or 'corporate' view of community' that is replacing the individualism or atomism of modernism.[31] This 'renewed sense of the importance and irreducibility of community' does not deny the significance of the individual; rather, the conception is that the individual cannot be understood apart from his or her role in the community.[32] As post-modernism's fresh understanding of, and emphasis on, community filters down to lived contemporary culture, it appears to augur well for a religious faith that is community-based. Thus, the Catholic Church should benefit significantly from this dimension of post-modernity. However, this will be determined by the model of Church that is operative. In the post-modern perspective, 'power is distributed more evenly, a plurality of viewpoints are appreciated and differences are celebrated.'[33]

If the post-modernists' understanding of community becomes fully embedded in contemporary culture, the issue will not be whether one is in or out of community. Rather, it will be a matter of deciding to which community one chooses to belong. Communities that are open to diversity will be more attractive to the post-modern sensibility, whereas communities that strive to be homogeneous will close themselves off from the diversity that is inherent in the post-modern thought and way of life.

The challenge facing the Catholic Church (and religious bodies generally) at the beginning of a new millennium is whether it can critically embrace the post-modernist perspective and its attending culture of post-modernity; whether it can embrace unity in diversity, allowing all viewpoints to be accorded value, while at the same time preserving the essential parameters of belief, structure, and practice; and whether it can continue the positive relationship between faith and culture that was initiated at Vatican II.

Religious Response to Modernity and Post-modernity

Dermot Lane notes that during the one hundred years between the First and Second Vatican Councils, the Catholic Church reacted against the rising post-Enlightenment culture of modernity. The underlying issue during this period concerned the relationship between the Church and the world, or more specifically, the relationship, or lack of it, between faith and culture. Lane says that 'the reaction of the Church to the winds of the modern world was one of withdrawal', leading to the emergence of a Catholic subculture in the nineteenth and early twentieth centuries.[34] DeLubac describes a

Catholic theology during this period in which 'the supernatural was exiled';[35] in other words, the realms of nature, history, and the secular were desacralized. It was not until the Second Vatican Council that the Church 'slowly but surely . . . embraced the culture of modernity for the first time.'[36]

The Catholic Church's response to modernity changed dramatically after the middle of the last century, as culture became a major theme at the Second Vatican Council. Indeed, the relationship between faith and culture became the central non-ecclesiological issue at the Second Vatican Council and in the Post-Conciliar Church. Not only was this the first time in Church history that an ecumenical council debated at length the concept of culture, but it devoted a major chapter to this theme in *Gaudium et spes*. Having dismissed a defensive and ahistorical text prepared by the Roman Curia, the bishops proceeded to view contemporary culture in a very positive light. The Pastoral Constitution on the Church stated that it 'is one of the marks of the human person to reach true and authentic humanity only through culture.'[37] Indeed the overall tone, and many of the statements in this document, had been considered almost heretical just a century earlier. In 1851, Pope Pius IX condemned the proposition that 'the Roman Pontiff can and should reconcile and harmonize himself with progress, with liberalism, and with recent civilization.'[38]

Apart from a brief period after the Council, when the focus was on atheism, cultural concerns have had a significant place in Catholic Church documents. The pontificate of Pope John Paul II, for example, has been characterized by unbroken attention to the topic of culture. He frequently calls for a new Christian culture and a new evangelization, as is illustrated in his 'Address to the Sixth Symposium of the Council of European Episcopal Conferences':

> The decline of ideologies, the erosion of confidence in the ability of structures to respond to the deeper problems and the anxious expectations of humanity, the dissatisfaction with an existence based on the ephemeral, the loneliness of the massive metropolises, the young abandoned to themselves, and nihilism itself have created a huge vacuum which awaits credible heralds of any new proposals of values capable of building any

civilization worthy of human vocation. . . . The Church is called to give a soul to modern society.

According to David Tracy, the challenge of post-modernity to Christian faith differs from that of modernity. He views post-modernity as a new sensibility, which is more open to Christian faith than modernity, the latter being characterized by a 'drive to sameness, the modern Western scientific, technological, democratic culture that is culture and history.'[39] Post-modernity is less arrogant and is more open to the mystical dimensions of religious experience. Gallagher, too, believes that 'a post-modern spirituality can be born that does justice both to the core relationship of faith, the radical concreteness of Christ and its prophetic challenges to our broken world… and to reopen the conversation about the ultimate goals of life.'[40] In this regard, Egan comments that

> The religious impulse will always reveal itself as a search for wholeness, as a longing for psychological and cultural individuality. Such preoccupations, never far away in modern writing, are the most obvious expression of the religious instinct in this turbulent century.[41]

Sharon Reed also refers to post-modernity's openness to the mystical dimensions of life when she writes that young people in particular yearn for 'a vision that is worthy of their time, attention and commitment.'[42] They hunger for leadership and community, for justice and the holy. There is significant evidence of this hunger for mystery when one works with adolescents and young adults. Currently, they desire an experience of meditative prayer in contrast to a decade or more ago when their primary interest was in rational discussion and debate, leaning toward a strong criticism of, or negative attitudes towards, religion. Significantly, going hand in hand with this spiritual hunger, there is clear evidence of a certain indifference towards, and even suspicion of, institutionalized religion among the younger generation. This may reflect what Doyle McCarthy describes as post-modernity's 'relentless relativism, the hostility to theory, and its suspicion of absolutes.'[43] In reference to two surveys of Irish Catholics

(1981 and 1990), which demonstrated a 20 per cent decrease in belief in a personal God and a 50 per cent increase in belief in God as 'some sort of Spirit or Life-force', Joseph Dunne remarked that

> There certainly seems to be a marked shift in the nature of what counts as 'religion' – a shift away from faith in a historically specific revelation, articulated theologically in doctrines such as the Trinity and the Incarnation, towards a more diffuse form of what might be called 'spirituality'.[44]

Nevertheless, the search for wholeness and for a meaningful spirituality, which can be seen among many young people as well as some adults, is at least open to, and offers the possibility of dialogue with, the Christian story and its institutionalized, symbolic, and liturgical expression.

Cultural Analysis and Discernment

Many current philosophers and theologians call for an aggressive discernment of contemporary Western culture, while others call for what is variously described as a new civil religion, common religion, political theology, public philosophy or public theology.[45] Gallagher uses strong words in his critique of contemporary culture. He speaks, for example, of the tyranny of images, of religious rootlessness, of faith deafness, of religious anaemia, and the seductive power of the prevailing culture. However, in considering three possible Christian responses to today's Western culture – tense hostility, innocent acceptance, discernment and creation of culture – Gallagher does not believe in playing the role of the 'tense adversary'. Rather, in considering the clashing symbols of faith and culture, he calls for gospel-rooted, aggressive discernment of every aspect of modern culture.[46]

John Kavanaugh represents, not only the school of aggressive discerners of contemporary culture, but also the school of the 'tense adversaries'. 'The way of Christ', he writes, 'is the way of freedom . . . His claim upon our lives is total; and it is in collision with our culture.'[47] In terms of Niebuhr's five categories of the relationship between Christianity and culture,[48] Kavanaugh stands very much in the 'Christ-against-Culture' camp as he resolutely rejects culture's claim to loyalty by the Christian. He draws on some insights from Karl Marx in his Christian critique of North American society, which he perceives to be characterized by rampant consumerism. This consumerist culture influences every dimension of people's lives and results in the loss of personhood – an eclipse that he blames on the philosophy of post-modernist thinkers. What he calls the Commodity Form of life is responsible for dehumanization and for the loss of interiority, and his view is that the authentic Christian response to this human predicament is conversion to the Personal Form. By this he means 'a mode of perceiving and valuing men and women as irreplaceable persons whose fundamental identities are fulfilled in covenantal relationships', the fullest revelation of which is found in Jesus Christ as we encounter him 'in history, tradition, Scripture, the communal endeavor of believers, and personal experience.'[49]

One of the characteristics of the impact of contemporary culture on Christianity is what one might call the reductionist tendency. What Gallagher calls the emasculation or acculturation of Christianity, and Metz describes as bourgeois religion, Kavanaugh refers to as the domestication of the Christian faith. He is concerned about people who have formal memberships of the Christian churches and yet follow the gospel of the culture. This is indeed an observable characteristic among all age groups, but especially among significant numbers of young people who choose to 'practise' Catholicism. Kavanaugh challenges all who profess belief in Jesus of Nazareth and belong to his community of disciples to become more aware of the ways in which their faith has become domesticated or acculturated. Metz is probably the most scathing of all on the issue. 'In the Christianity of our time', he writes, 'the messianic religion of the Bible has been largely changed into bourgeois religion.'[50] A prophetic critique of this form of Christianity is more urgent than ever before. Groome also warns about the danger of the Christian community merely reflecting society and he calls for a dialectical relationship between the faith community and its cultural context, as well as a dialectical relationship between the faith community and its individual members in order to promote the continual reformation of the Church.[51]

In the dynamic of Western culture and Christian faith, particularly as it is institutionalized in the Catholic Church, there is a crucial role for symbols as carriers of culture. One of the challenges facing Christianity today is that contemporary cultural symbols are replacing religious symbols. Evidence of this can be seen in the celebration of the Sacraments of Initiation in the Catholic Church. Parents for whom the religious symbolism of these significant moments in their children's lives has lost its meaning, reinvest these occasions with new meaning through contemporary cultural symbols. In answer to this problem of faith being co-opted by culture, Kavanaugh states that 'the life of Jesus . . . his saving action . . . his people and its traditions, all offer a most stunning contrast to cultural idols.'[52] In this regard, the question today is not so much, 'Do you believe in God?', but rather, 'What God do you believe in?'

In turning specifically to the impact of contemporary Western culture on the beliefs, values, and practices of adolescents and young adults, one may safely say that what applies to the general population applies *par excellence* to the younger generation, particularly as the latter is more affected by the technological revolution and more passive towards, and uncritical of, the values communicated through the powerful, fast-moving media world of images.

Cultural analysis and discernment is probably the most difficult and ambitious goal of youth ministry today. As has been noted above, Kavanaugh's analysis focuses on the social trends in contemporary culture. Warren, on the other hand, gives much attention to viewing the scene from the point of view of communications and youth ministry. Warren agrees with Kavanaugh in the belief that we should not be too naive about cultural control and oppression today. They both see contemporary Western culture as undermining, not only Church-related Christian faith, but the requisite openness that is necessary for believing, especially among the younger generation. This perception is very similar to Gallagher's notion of 'faith-deafness' referred to earlier.

In understanding discernment of culture as involving patterns of interpreting reality, Warren is of the opinion that 'people do not so much believe in their society's patterns of thought and feeling; they approach life by means of them.'[53] If one accepts this interpretation, it follows that 'culture offers assumptions that become the unnoticed and pre-reflective paradigms which people live by.'[54] One of Warren's most valuable insights is that faith today cannot be alive and genuinely Christian unless it becomes alert to the cultural values and meanings that shape people's attitudes into what he calls 'structures of feeling'. The real issue here is an undermining of the possibility of faith because of a lack of freedom, with the result that young people are not ready for the gospel. Therefore, Warren concludes that 'coming to see that one has a way of seeing involves a shift of consciousness and for many this shift will be mediated through artful explanation.'[55]

Clearly, there is much work to be done in this regard by those who would assist young people in learning how to deal with the image systems of culture. Kavanaugh follows a similar line of thought when he recognizes that a first step towards Christian faith entails realizing the pervasiveness of what he describes as the 'commodity form'. Only in this way can one come to realize inevitable 'oppositions between cultural wisdom and Christian wisdom.'[56] Other commentators share similar views regarding the cultural challenges to the possibility of genuine Christian faith among young people and, consequently, among the next generation of adults. Tonelli offers this view:

> The current challenge in youth ministry is not religious but anthropological: it is about who they are becoming. This question of identity requires a prior critique of the manipulative images of the dominant culture.[57]

There is a growing awareness today of the importance of imagination for religious faith. Christian faith involves the 'heart' much more than the 'head' of the believer. This, indeed, was recognized a century ago, even though it has received little attention until recent decades. John Henry Newman believed that 'the heart is commonly reached not through reason but through imagination.'[58] A major problem with the multi-media culture is that excessive, passive viewing of the visual media is congealing childrens' and young peoples' imaginations. Current statistics indicate that by the end of secondary school, the present generation of youth will have spent more time watching television than they will have spent in class. This has the overall effect of diminishing their imaginative potential, medicating their feelings, dulling their sensitivities, and numbing their interior lives. Diarmuid O'Murchu makes the comment that

> The inability to think deeply and imaginatively is one of the most serious social, cultural and spiritual deprivations of the contemporary world. In the West, particularly, we are conditioned into being linear, rational robots, starved of the capacity for imaginative and creative reflection.[59]

Andrew Greeley also refers to the importance of imagination for faith. 'Primordially', he says, 'religion is a function of the creative imagination.'[60] This leads some people to conclude that the crisis of faith among many young people is, perhaps, not in the area of doctrine or creeds but in that of sensibility or imagination. 'It is on the preconceptual level of intuitive activity – called imagination – that religious meaning is encountered and explored.'[61]

In reviewing the literature on the overall impact of contemporary Western culture on Christian faith, one might be tempted to conclude that the scales weigh heavily against the survival of institutionalized Christian faith in the future, especially among the young. However, while it is important to face reality, there should be no pessimism among those concerned with either the evangelization of contemporary culture or its inhabitants. In the words of the Canadian Catholic philosopher, Charles Taylor, 'one has to see what is great in the culture of modernity, as well as what is shallow and dangerous.'[62] One must be careful to avoid one of the two perennial tendencies in Catholicism described by John Courtney Murray, the attitude of contempt for the world, since this leads ultimately to the rejection of the cultural enterprise. It is good to remember that 'the question of Christianity and civilization is by no means a new one; that Christian perplexity in this area has been perennial and that the problem has been an enduring one through all the Christian centuries.'[63] Of the five typical Christian answers to the relationship of Christianity to culture that are offered by Neibhur – Christ against Culture, Christ of Culture, Christ above Culture, Christ and Culture in Paradox, Christ the Transformer of Culture – it seems that the most appropriate response to the culture of this age is to understand Christianity as a transforming agency within contemporary culture. This requires of the committed Christian a positive hope-filled attitude toward culture and belongs, as Niebuhr points out, 'to the great central tradition of the Church.'[64]

Notes

1. E. Doyle McCarthy, *Knowledge as Culture: The New Sociology of Knowledge* (London: Routledge, 1996), p. 1.
2. Ibid., p. 5.
3. M. Warren, *Communications and Cultural Analysis* (Westport CT: Bergin and Garvey, 1992), p. 6.
4. P. Schineller, *A Handbook on Inculturation* (Mahwah, NJ: Paulist Press, 1990), p. 22.
5. E. B. Tylor, *Primitive Culture,* vol. 1 (London: John Murray, 1871), p. 1.
6. E. Doyle McCarthy, op. cit., p. 104.
7. M. P. Gallagher, *Clashing Symbols: An Introduction to Faith and Culture* (London: Darton, Longman & Todd, 1997), p. 13.
8. C. Geertz, *The Interpretation of Cultures* (New York: Basic Books, 1973), p. 89.
9. E. Doyle McCarthy, op. cit., p. 20.
10. C. Geertz, op. cit., p. 5.
11. A. L. Kroeber and D. Kluckhohn, *Culture: A Critical Review of Concepts and Definitions* (New York: Vintage Books, 1983).
12. A. Shorter, *Towards a Theology of Inculturation* (New York: Orbis Books, 1988), p. 5.
13. Ibid., p. 20.
14. T. H. Groome, 'Postmodernism: The Challenges and Opportunities for Religious Education.' Paper presented at the annual meeting of the APRRE Conference (Orlando, Florida, November 1998), p. 1.
15. V. A. Harvey, *The Historian and the Believer: The Morality of Historical Knowledge and Christian Belief* (New York: Macmillan, 1996).
16. R. M. Gula, *Reason Informed by Faith: Foundations of Catholic Morality* (New York: Paulist Press, 1989), p. 32.
17. Ibid., p. 33.
18. B. Lonergan, *A Second Collection.* W. F. J. Ryan and B. J. Tyrrell, eds. (Philadelphia: The Westminster Press, 1974), p. 58.
19. Ibid., p. 57.

20. Ibid., p. 59.
21. D. Tracy, *Blessed Rage for Order: The New Pluralism in Theology* (New York: Seabury Press, 1975), p. 10.
22. M. P. Gallagher, op. cit., p. 67.
23. Ibid., p. 73.
24. E. Doyle McCarthy, op. cit., p. 108.
25. Ibid., p. 71.
26. M. P. Gallagher, op. cit., p. 71.
27. C. Taylor, *The Ethics of Authenticity* (Cambridge, MA: Harvard University Press, 1991).
28. Groome, op. cit., p. 1.
29. T. E. Leuze, 'Is Shared Christian Praxis Postmodern? An Anglo-American Postmodern Consideration.' Paper presented at the APRRE Annual Meeting (Orlando, Florida, 1998).
30. J. Gill, *Learning to Learn: Towards a Philosophy of Education* (Atlantic Highlands, NJ: Humanities Press International, 1993), p. 48.
31. N. Murphy, *Anglo American Postmodernity: Philosophical Perspectives on Science, Religion and Ethics* (Boulder, CO: Westview Press, 1997), p. 6.
32. N. Murphy, *Theology in the Age of Scientific Reasoning* (Ithaca, NY: Cornell University Press, 1990), p. 201.
33. Leuze, op. cit., p. 155.
34. D. Lane, *Religion and Culture in Dialogue* (Dublin: Columba Press, 1993), p. 15.
35. H. de Lubac, *The Christian Resistance to Anti-Semitism: Memoirs from 1940–1944* (San Francisco: Ignatius Press, 1990), p. 19–21.
36. Lane, op. cit., p. 14.
37. *Pastoral Constitution on the Church,* No. 53.
38. *Syllabus of Errors,* Proposition 80, cited in Lane, 1993.
39. D. Tracy, 'Theology and the Many Faces of Postmodernity', *Theology Today* 51 (1994), p. 107.
40. Gallagher, op. cit., pp. 96–97.
41. J. Egan, *The Death of Metaphor* (Newbridge: The Kavanagh Press, 1990), p. 113.
42. S. Reid, ed., *Spirituality* (New Rochelle NY: Don Bosco Multimedia, 1991).
43. E. Doyle McCarthy, op. cit., p. 102.

44. J. Dunne, 'Religion and Modernity: Reading the Signs', in *Faith and Culture in the Irish Context,* ed. E. G. Cassidy (Dublin: Veritas Publications, 1996), p. 121.

45. L. S. Rouner, ed., *Civil Religion and Political Theology* (Notre Dame, IN: Notre Dame Press, 1986).

46. Gallagher, op. cit., pp. 123–124.

47. J. F. Kavanaugh, *Following Christ in a Consumer Society* (New York: Orbis Books, 1991), p. xiv.

48. H. R. Niebuhr, *Christ and Culture* (New York: Harper and Row, 1951).

49. Kavanaugh, op. cit., p. 65.

50. J. B. Metz, *The Emergent Church: The Future of Christianity in a Postbourgeois World,* trans. P. Mann (New York: Crossroads, 1981), pp. 1–2.

51. T. H. Groome, *Christian Religious Education: Sharing Our Story and Vision* (San Francisco: Harper and Row, 1980), p. 107.

52. Kavanaugh, op. cit., p. xiii.

53. Warren, op. cit., p. 143.

54. Gallagher, op. cit., p. 129.

55. Warren, op. cit., p. 118.

56. Kavanaugh, op. cit., p. 165.

57. R. Tonelli, (cited in Gallagher 1997).

58. J. H. Newman, *Grammar of Assent* (London: Longman, 1901), p. 92.

59. D. Ó Murchu, *Reclaiming Spirituality: A New Spiritual Framework for Today's World* (Dublin: Gill and Macmillan, 1997), p. 6.

60. A. Greeley, *Religion: A Secular Theory* (New York: Transaction, 1982), p. 48.

61. Gallagher, op. cit., p. 116.

62. Taylor, op. cit., p. 120.

63. Niebuhr, op. cit., p. 2.

64. Ibid., p. 190.

CHAPTER III

FAITH AND CULTURE IN THE IRISH CONTEXT

In order to fully appreciate and understand the changes in beliefs and values among Irish youth, one has to be sensitive to the larger picture. Thus, it is in the context of the emerging cultural patterns in the Western world generally, that the unique Irish situation regarding the changing patterns of Catholic faith and practice is addressed. It is equally important to keep in mind that the expression of faith, which was universal in Ireland until three decades ago, was a reflection of the cultural legacy that is Irish history. Michael Drumm argues that 'only when due weight is given to the historical and theological consequences' of the Great Hunger of 1845–1848 'can an adequate interpretation of many characteristics of the contemporary dialogue of faith and culture in the Irish context be provided.'[1] He goes on to ask the question: 'Why for one hundred years did Irish Catholics, both at home and in the diaspora, maintain a level of church attendance which seems unparalleled in history?' In answering this question, he analyzes the effects of the Famine of 1845–1848 on the religious consciousness of Irish Catholics.

For many centuries prior to the Famine, Irish Catholicism was characterized by a rich blend of Celtic spirituality and 'orthodox' Christianity. This living incarnate religion was ritualized very often outside the confines of Church buildings and centered around four great feasts, marking the beginning of the four seasons of the year. The first challenge to this unique expression of Christianity, integrated into the lives of Irish Catholics, came from what Drumm calls 'the violent iconoclastic forces of the Reformation.' This was followed by the Counter-Reformation, which 'sought to restructure the Catholic Church through purging many traditional practices in the embrace of an essentially clerical ecclesial vision.'

Throughout the eighteenth century, the Catholic Church devoted much energy to the creation of Church structures, especially parishes, and also to catechesis on the sacraments and doctrinal formation. As Bridget McCormack's recent research has demonstrated, sermons on St Patrick, 'as the icon of Irish Catholicism' were one of the means used to communicate 'the tenets of the Tridentine Church to the laity.'[2] For example, in the sermons of a prominent Franciscan preacher, William Gahan, there was a clear shift away from the account of miracles and wonder-working that had hitherto been associated with Patrick. Instead, 'Gahan's message to the *pobail Dé* (people of God) bore the hallmarks of the Tridentine image of sanctity.' He emphasized the importance of prayer and the reception of the sacraments and made no reference whatsoever to the great miracles that were characteristic of traditional Patrician preaching. Thus, even the long-standing image of Ireland's national patron changed as a result of the new catechesis.

During the second half of the eighteenth century, the Catholic hierarchy issued many letters and pastorals requesting that the clergy refrain from joining the people in pilgrimages to holy wells and other places of devotion. Furthermore, they were to discourage patrons and pilgrimages generally. Above all, they were instructed not to say Mass at these events as had been the practice hitherto. The place for Mass, the clergy were told, was in the chapel. In spite of clerical opinions and admonishments, McCormack's research reveals that toward the end of the eighteenth century, Irish Catholics had continued to adhere to their ancient spirituality. There is clear evidence, she says, that 'popular practices still lingered, even in clerical quarters, despite the appeals and efforts of the hierarchy.' Even the popular cult surrounding Patrick was only slightly dented by clerical reform and the Catholic Church was faced with a dilemma regarding the patron saint. The strength of the cult prevented the effective use of the image of Patrick in the preaching of a reformed message within more regulated surroundings. However, 'the groundwork for the divergence of popular religious practice and church worship had been laid by the attempt to dissociate sacramental devotion from the patrons.'

It is clear that by the middle of the nineteenth century, despite the best efforts of Church and English-ruled State to 'purify' religion, the Irish people held to their ancient ritual celebrations with great tenacity. It required one of the greatest peace-time catastrophes to change that.

Where the Reformation and Counter-Reformation had failed, the Famine succeeded in transforming the religious minds and hearts of Irish Catholics. 'It is in this sense', says Drumm, 'that it is probably true to speak of contemporary Irish Catholicism as a post-Famine phenomenon.'[3] Traditional rituals were relentlessly attacked by both Catholic priests and Protestant evangelists. Their path was cleared, as there were no longer any first fruits of the harvest to celebrate the feast of Lughnasa (August 1).

The second attempt at a Protestant Reformation in Ireland, in post-Famine years, was met face to face with a Counter-Reformation. The former failed, whereas the latter had extraordinary success under the leadership of Paul Cullen, Archbishop of Dublin. Drumm remarks that 'the effect of Cullen on the post-Famine Church is so enormous that some have termed it the Cullenisation of Irish Catholicism.' Larkin describes the changes that occurred in the decades following the Great Hunger as nothing less than a 'devotional revolution'.[4] As Bailey points out, people were weaned 'from an over-reliance on elements of folk religion to a chapel-centered practice of faith.'[5] By 1870 it became clear that the Cullen reforms were triumphant and, in the words of Larkin, the 'great mass of Irish people became practicing Catholics'[6] and have uniquely remained so both at home and in the diaspora until recent decades.

The success of the new version of Irish Catholicism was in no small part due to the influence of the clergy as the primary community leaders of a people whose spirit had been broken by the Great Hunger. Commentators agree that the post-Famine Church leaders could not have foreseen the full extent of the success of their programme. The first half of the twentieth century witnessed an extraordinary rise in vocations to the priesthood and religious life, together with a very expansive missionary drive throughout the world. This was also the Irish religio-cultural story up to the 1960s. Thereafter, it was evident that the Catholic Church in Ireland, now heavily influenced by traditional European structures, would have great difficulty in responding to the rapid socio-economic and cultural change that was about to occur and permeate every level of Irish society. What Yeats could once describe as the village-style 'unity of culture' has broken apart with its attendant implications for Christian faith lived in community.

Economic, Social, and Cultural Change in Ireland

In 1958, few Irish people could have realized the extraordinary impact that the Programme for Economic Expansion would have on the Republic of Ireland. At this time, Irish society could be characterized as pre-modern. Perched in the Atlantic Ocean, off the West coast of the European mainland, Ireland had neither experienced the Enlightenment nor the Industrial Revolution. The escape from the former had more to do with the Famine than with geographical isolation. Drumm points out that

> The Enlightenment did not influence Irish Catholics because the Famine had turned their hearts and minds in a different direction – not towards the rights of the individual, freedom of inquiry, respect for the emerging sciences and progress; but towards survival, tenant rights, emigration and fear of what life might hold.[7]

Following the Programme for Economic Expansion, industrialization proceeded at a very rapid rate and, as a consequence, quite phenomenal social change occurred. But unlike Europe and North America, a century was crammed into thirty years. Ireland, in line with the Western world generally, experienced the shadow side of modernity but, 'because of the rapidity of the changes . . . and because of the quite different points of departure, the shadows can seem deeper and longer.'[8] Now, with the fastest growing economy in Europe, Ireland's revolutionary economic change has brought about very rapid social change which, in turn, is effecting cultural change. This is having a particular impact on young people.

Cassidy reminds us of 'the complexity of the task of understanding the changing patterns of faith and practice' in an Irish cultural climate that has altered almost beyond recognition in three decades.[9] Up to the 1960s, the extraordinary success of the Post-Famine religious renewal, matched by a residue of Celtic spirituality that was characterized by a strong sense of a Divine Presence permeating everything, ensured that religious belief and practice were seamlessly woven into a whole pattern of life in a predominantly rural society. The initial gradual, and then rapid, decline in religious practice cannot be understood without taking into account the disintegration of the wider cultural fabric that was still relatively intact in Ireland up to the 1960s.

As Ireland has experienced very significant socio-cultural change and become increasingly secularized, there has been a corresponding weakening of religious beliefs among many people, particularly the young. Whelan and Fahey argue that

> Young people have been less and less successfully socialized into institutional religion as Ireland has moved from a position of 'moral monopoly' to de facto pluralism, where there is ready access to multiple media sources, values and lifestyles.[10]

In addition, 'there are indications that a major cultural shift may have occurred for those born in recent decades.'[11] This observation was echoed some four years ago when a group of adults, representing almost every parish in an Irish diocese, as well as a representative number of clergy, gathered to reflect on their experience of Church at parish, diocesan, and national levels. One of the most prominent issues that surfaced in small-group reports concerned the crisis of faith among young people. The experience reflected by this Assembly was that the Catholic Church in Ireland is rapidly losing its youth, and that without some appropriate intervention, this exodus will accelerate. The official report on this diocesan Assembly pointed out that the crisis of faith among the rising generation was perceived as one of the greatest challenges facing the Catholic Church in Ireland today. In particular, participants felt that young members of the Church 'form their own culture and their own attitudes and decide for themselves.' Furthermore, 'the Church is experienced as being in transition, but is not adapting quickly enough'.[12]

The power of social life to affect meanings, values, attitudes, and behaviour is referred to by Doyle McCarthy: 'Social life does not stop at the doors of our being, but passes into the chambers of our minds and psyches, and insinuates itself even into the domain of spoken and unspoken thoughts and desires. Social life is not an aspect, but the environment of human being.'[13]

Just as economic change always brings about social change, so also the latter inevitably effects significant cultural shifts. It is important, therefore, to distinguish between society and culture. Social change is visible and can be measured, whereas cultural change is less visible. It is concerned with meaning, values and attitudes. Thus, in order to understand cultural change, one needs to look at the change that occurs at the level of meaning and values resulting from social change.

New Waves of Religious Change

This section examines various statistics that reflect the religious change that has occurred in Ireland during the 1970s and 1980s. The results of the various scientific surveys that were carried out during this period demonstrate a surprisingly small change in religious practice. As will be seen later, it was not until the 1990s that very rapid changes occurred in this regard. There is a certain validity in Joseph Dunne's reservations regarding quantitative surveys in that 'the questions asked of the respondents are formulated in terms of a small number of precoded categories, so that a great deal of nuance or differentiating detail is forfeit *ab initio*', without any opportunity for 'dialogical exchange between respondent and questioner which might evoke a reflective attitude.'[14] Nevertheless, statistics regarding religious belief and practice that come from scientific surveys do demonstrate changing patterns. In particular, Cassidy believes that 'the European Values Surveys represent a thorough investigation into Irish social mores and are generally regarded as the authoritative barometers of social change in contemporary Ireland.'[15]

The report of the first national survey on religious belief and practice in 1974 provided evidence that, on average, 91% of Irish people attended Mass at least once per week.[16] Ten years later, a similar national survey on behalf of the Research and Development Unit of the Irish Catholic Church, showed a drop of 4% in weekly Mass attendance – down to 87%.[17] MacGreil's report on the results of interviews with a random sample of 1,005 respondents in 1988–1989 demonstrates that the weekly Mass attendance dropped by another 5% to 82%. He remarks that 'the decline of 9% in (national) weekly Mass attendance over a period of fifteen years is significant but not very substantial, that is, less than 1% per annum.'[18] He notes, however, that 'during the period 1984–89, the rate of annual decline had reached 1% per annum, which is more than twice the annual decline of 0.4% per annum during the period 1974–84.' As can be seen from the 1988/1989 survey (Table 1) there has been quite a dramatic decline in

| Frequency of Sacramental Practice of Roman Catholics (Republic of Ireland) 1974, 1984, and 1988/1989 | | | | | |
| | | | Differences | | |
	1974 A	1984 B	1988/ 1989 C	A-B (10 years)	B-C (5 years)	A-C (15 years)
1. Weekly Mass Attendance	91%	87%	82%	-4%	-5%	-9%
2a. Weekly Holy Communion	28%	38%	43%	+10%	+5%	+15%
2b. Monthly Holy Communion	66%	64%	63%	-2%	-1%	-3%
3. Monthly Confession	47%	26%	18%	-21%	-8%	-29%
N	2499	1006	1005			

Table 1

the frequency with which people celebrate sacramental confession. MacGreil notes that 'such a rate of decline clearly indicates a change of norm among Roman Catholics in the Republic of Ireland.'

Table 2 examines participation in formal worship according to age and area of rearing. It is interesting to note here that the youngest age category (18–20 years old) records a higher level of participation than does the 21–35 year-old sample. This is probably accounted for by the fact that the younger age group are more closely linked with home than the over 21 age group. MacGreil points to the fact that area of rearing and county of residence 'clearly indicate the negative effect of urbanization on formal religious practice.'

The reasons given for not attending Mass weekly are included in Table 3. As one can see from the table, indifference is by far the biggest single reason for less frequent attendance at weekly formal worship. This reflects a certain apathy, which has been referred to earlier as one of the characteristics of postmodernism.

Whelan and Fahey present evidence from the European Values Surveys of 1981 and 1990 on religious values and behaviour in Ireland

and comment on its significance for the Catholic Church. They note that 'the period covered by the surveys in question does not include the revelations of clerical misbehavior which has rocked the Catholic Church in Ireland' in the last number of years.[19] However, they point

Mass Attendance (of Roman Catholics) by Age, Area of Rearing, and County of Residence					
Personal Variable	Weekly or more often	1–3 times a month or more often	Several times a year or more often	Less often or never	N
A. Age (p < .001)					
1. 18-20 years	78%	84%	98%	2%	55
2. 21-35 years	71%	81%	92%	8%	320
3. 36 -50 years	88%	90%	94%	6%	246
4. 51 years	90%	92%	95%	5%	319
B. Area of rearing (p < .001)					
1. Large City (1000,000+)	64%	73%	87%	13%	203
2. Small City (10,000+)	77%	87%	91%	9%	106
3. Town (1500)	86%	90%	94%	6%	142
4. Rural	89%	92%	97%	3%	487
C. County of residence (p < .001)					
1. Dublin (County and City)	69%	76%	90%	10%	251
2. Rest of Leinster	78%	86%	93%	7%	238
3. Munster	90%	93%	97%	3%	286
4. Connaught/Ulster	92%	95%	96%	4%	166
Total sample	82%	87%	94%	6%	941

Table 2

out that it does relate to a period in which a deep unease about the future of religion had become quite marked in religious circles in Ireland. A sharp decline in religious vocations, the increasingly liberal and secular cast of many developments in public policy, the virtual abandonment by many Catholics of tenets of their religion having to do with reproductive and sexual morality, and a more questioning attitude towards Church authority were among the causes of that unease.

Reasons for Not Attending Mass 'At Least Once A Week'		
Reason	Subsample	Percentage of Total Sample
1. Just don't bother	62%	10.9
2. Working	10%	1.8
3. Complaint about Faith	7%	1.2
4. Ill	6%	1.1
5. Distance from place of Worship	3%	0.5
6. Other reasons	12%	2.2
	N = 179	17.7

Table 3

As well as providing evidence of the pace and extent of change in religious adherence generally, Whelan and Fahey identify subgroups in the population where change is most notable. This gives some appreciation of how forces such as age, education, unemployment, urbanization, and gender impact on institutionalized Christian faith. Figure 1 shows that Church attendance declines by age in the general population, but more especially among the urban dwellers – as low as 56% for those in their late twenties and early thirties. Figure 2

indicates the effect of gender and urban-rural location on weekly
Church attendance. One can observe here that it is mainly in urban
areas that males have a lesser tendency to attend Mass with the figure
falling to 65% in contrast to 87% for men in rural areas.

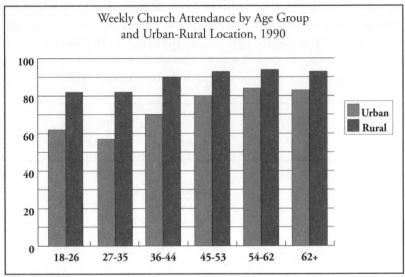

Figure 1

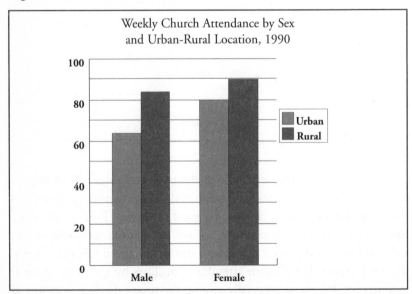

Figure 2

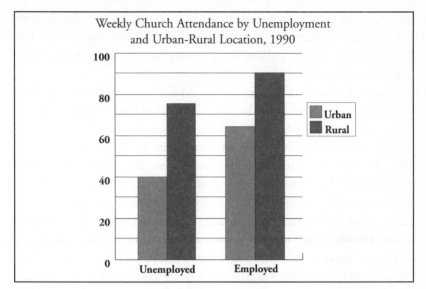

Figure 3

Figure 3 demonstrates that, just as in the case of gender, urban-rural location plays a significant role in mediating the impact of unemployment. Stronger community support probably accounts for the high percentage of weekly Church attendance among the unemployed in rural areas (75%) in contrast to the low rate of 40% in urban areas where social integration is likely to be weaker.

Whelan and Fahey introduce another factor that interacts with location and which they describe as 'basic life-style deprivation'. They say that 'there is no difference in the frequency of church attendance in rural areas between those experiencing such deprivation and other people', whereas in urban areas 'Church attendance is substantially reduced by such deprivation.' According to the Economic and Social Research Institute's poverty project, there is a strong link between employment and self-esteem, whereby those who are in full-time employment have access to a wide variety of experiences and social activities that are crucial to maintaining self-esteem.[20] On the other hand, the results of the ESRI poverty survey show that the unemployed are more likely to have a sense of worthlessness and less likely to feel that they have a useful part to play in social life. Commenting on these findings, Whelan and Fahey say that it is 'hardly surprising that the unemployed are less likely to participate in community rituals such as church attendance' and they also note that 'such findings lend no support to the compensatory view of religion.'

Figure 4 shows that there is very little variation in weekly Mass attendance by social class. In the 1990 European Values Study, six social classes were distinguished. Married women were allocated to the class of their husbands because of what Breen and Whelan point to as the absence of sufficient information for alternative satisfactory procedures.[21] Whelan and Fahey point out that 'the weakness of the social class effect is contributed to by the fact that primary life-style deprivation makes its strongest impact outside the unskilled manual class.' However, as Figure 4 shows, there is a significant interaction between social class and age, with 94% of the non-manual respondents attending Church weekly in contrast to 84% of the manual group. It is interesting to note that for those under forty, the pattern is reversed, indicating a new trend in religious practice.

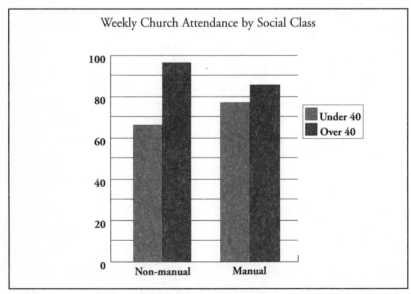

Figure 4

There is a definite interaction between age and higher levels of education:

> While on average only two-thirds of those with third-level education attended weekly, compared with over four-fifths of those with lower levels of education, the effect is almost entirely to be found among those born since the early 1950s. Once again it is apparent that significant cultural shifts can be dated from around the 1960s.[22]

This correlation between the decline in Church attendance with university or third-level education is ominous for the Catholic Church in Ireland, as the numbers of young people attending universities and third-level institutions of various kinds are increasing dramatically. Furthermore, it is current educational policy to achieve at least a 90% graduation rate from second-level education. Presently, the vast majority of secondary school graduates enter some form of third-level education. If Ireland follows the pattern of trends in the United States, as reported by Yankelovich, the values of the university students will filter through the youth population as a whole by way of what he calls 'cultural diffusion'.[23]

Table 4 shows that Catholics are much less distinctive in relation to confidence in the Church than in their religious behaviour and beliefs. For example, only 43% feel that the Church gives adequate answers to

Percentage of Catholics Who Consider that the Church Gives Adequate Answers to Problems	
	%
Individual's moral problems	43
Problems of family life	38
People's spiritual needs	70
Social problems	28

Table 4

an individual's moral problems. The only high score recorded was in the case of the Catholic Church's ability to meet people's spiritual needs.

According to the European Values Survey, apart from the Netherlands, Ireland scores lowest in relation to people's confidence in the Church to meet the moral problems of the individual. This is quite extraordinary when one considers that the same 1990 European Values Survey demonstrates that the average weekly Church attendance in Ireland was 80%, in contrast to the rest of Europe's average of 30%. It points to the Irish Catholic Church's inadequacy in responding to the moral, familial, and social problems of its people, despite its weekly opportunity to address the majority of them.

An interesting feature of Whelan and Fahey's analysis of the 1990 European Values Survey is that they regard the issue of feminism as one of the cultural developments in recent decades that has posed serious challenges to traditional Christian views of the world. They cite the collapse of female religious vocations, not only in Ireland, but in many parts of the Western world, as 'one indication of how new thinking about women's roles have helped to create a uniform outcome in religious behaviour across quite diverse societies in the West.'[24] (My own experience of working in an Irish university would seem to bear this out.) Young women are increasingly critical of what they regard as a patriarchal, male-dominated Church. Enda McDonagh comments that 'where the priest and the poet, in different ways and at different times, might have seemed central figures in Irish society, and the women . . . marginal, a radical change has occurred in principle and in practice.'[25] In further commenting on the looming marginal status of religion in Ireland, he states that 'for many people, it has been replaced as a source of spiritual and moral energy by the arts, and justice movements like the women's movement.'

Rapid Waves of Religious Change

Taken together, the surveys of Nic Chiolla Phadraig (1974), Breslin and Weaver (1984), MacGreil (1988/1989), and the European Values Surveys for which the data were collected in 1981 and 1990 show a significant, but not very substantial, decline in weekly Church attendance – 9% according to MacGreil and 10% according to

Whelan and Fahey. It appears from this evidence that despite the rapid socio-cultural change that had occurred in the previous two decades, by 1990 religious adherence was still very high in Ireland, at least by the standards of Western countries generally. The most notable lower allegiance is to be found among the post-1950s generation and especially at the two ends of the social spectrum – young, unemployed urban males on the one hand, and the university educated on the other.

On the basis of the findings presented in the above surveys there is little evidence of an overall disenchantment with the Catholic Church in Ireland up to the late 1980s (even if its authority has weakened considerably) despite rapid economic, social, and cultural change. The only significant behavioural and cultural shifts have occurred among the young, those with third-level education and those living in urban areas, especially the unemployed. Although empirical evidence is sparse between 1990 and 1998, the most recent surveys indicate that a rapid decline in religious affiliation has occurred in the 1990s. This is especially evident among the younger generation.

In July 1997, the Catholic Church Hierarchy's Council for Research and Development commissioned Irish Marketing Surveys (IMS) to question 1,400 men and women, fifteen years of age and upward, throughout the Republic of Ireland, about their religious beliefs and practices. The survey was carried out in July and September of that year. The research was conducted as part of the IMS Omnibus Survey, which is designed to be representative of the population aged fifteen years and over living in the Republic of Ireland.

The key findings of the IMS survey reveal that Mass attendance for the Catholic population as a whole has declined significantly during the last decade, down from 80% in 1990 to 65% in September 1997. This decline has accelerated rapidly in those seven years in contrast to the period between 1974 and 1990 when it was quite gradual. Age, and to a lesser extent, area of residence has the greatest impact on attendance at Mass. Approximately half of the 15–34 age bracket participate in the Eucharist at least once a week compared with more than 8 in 10 who are aged 50 years or older. Furthermore, when age and area of residence are taken together, the results are even more striking, if not shocking: only 31% of 25–34 year-old male, and 37%

of 25–34 year-old female urban dwellers go to Mass once a week, compared with 39% of 15–24 year-old male and 32% of 15–24 year-old female urban residents. One may conclude from these statistics that the majority of urban youth have abandoned a part of Irish culture that was virtually universal in their parents' generation.

Regular sacramental confession has been a strong feature of Irish Catholic life, especially since the Cullen reform in the post-famine years. The IMS survey reveals that participation in this sacrament has continued its dramatic decline since the 1970s when almost half of the Catholic population went to Confession at least once a month. In 1997, this figure had fallen to just over 1 in 10 Catholics (11%). During the same period, the number of those attending Mass who received Holy Communion continued to rise. This may be indicative of a changing sense of sin but is more likely an implicit challenge to the authority of the Catholic Church. Young people, in particular, do not experience the need to go through an intermediary in acknowledging their desire for God's forgiveness and may even resent the interference of Church officials in their private lives.

The IMS survey was the first to test the pulse of Irish Catholicism since a series of 'scandals' shook the Catholic Church in Ireland during the early to mid-1990s, receiving vast media coverage. Taking the survey population as a whole, 24% felt that the recent 'scandals' in Ireland did have a negative effect on their religious belief and practice. While the perceived negative impact of these events was felt across the board regardless of age, gender, or religion, it was more marked among the younger generation, especially those in their twenties. However, the greatest impact would appear to have been on those Catholics whose affiliation to the Church in terms of sacramental participation was below average. When the first wave of recent 'scandals' broke, there was widespread media speculation that this would lead to a mass exodus of people from the Church. Hence, there was a sense of relief and surprise among the leadership when the IMS survey revealed that 72% of the respondents claimed that their religious belief and practice had not been affected. One may conclude from this that the changing patterns of belief and practice are primarily the result of the unprecedented social and cultural change that is sweeping the Irish landscape and particularly affecting the rising generation.

Active Church membership is traditionally measured by participation in the Eucharist and sacramental Confession. Tables 5 and 6 capture the current situation regarding Church affiliation for the population as a whole. While the focus of this book is on young

Frequency of Attending Mass, Confession, and Holy Communion		
	Mass %	Confession %	Holy Communion %
Daily	4	--	4
More than once a week and holy days	5	--	4
Once a week	57	--	34
Twice or three times a month	2	1	5
Once a month	7	8	9
About six times a year	3	12	8
2-3 times a year	2	21	5
Only rarely	5	19	10
Special occasions only (i.e. Christmas, Easter)	5	11	8
Never	9	25	16

Note. Base: All Roman Catholics (N = 1,311) -- 15 + years.

Table 5

Reasons for Going to Mass Less Often Nowadays	
	%
No interest/boring	18
Less faith because of scandals	17
Too awkward/too much hassle/no transport	13
No particular reason	9
Don't have the time/Work weekends/exams	8
Getting too old/ill health	8
Not religious/do not believe/do not agree with Mass	7
Move out of home/Made to go by parents when younger	4
More relaxed/forget to go	3
Kids	3
Don't like attitude of Church	2
Friends/family don't go anymore	2
Note. Base: All saying go less often nowadays (n=242.)	

Table 6

people, it is important to remember that a decline in Church commitment by the general adult population supports the accelerating decline in religious disaffection among youth.

As was the case in previous surveys, the major reason given for going to Mass less often was boredom and lack of interest. However, this time a new element was introduced, namely, the effect of the recent 'scandals' involving Church personnel. This category of people vied with those who were disinterested.

Regarding confidence in Church leadership, 29% of the surveyed population reported that the 'scandals' affected their confidence in the priests of their parish and 26% said that confidence in the bishop of their own diocese had been adversely affected. This means that a majority did not lose faith in Church leadership as a result of this issue.

The second major survey conducted in recent times to take the pulse of Irish Catholicism occurred in January 1998. This was a non-Church initiative and was commissioned by the national television network. RTE's *Prime Time* programme commissioned the Market Research Bureau of Ireland (MRBI) to conduct a similar survey to that of the IMS. Questions relating to religious belief and practice were again asked of a somewhat smaller, but representative, group of people in the Republic of Ireland. These were aged eighteen and upwards and surveyed at one hundred locations throughout the State.

Ann Hanley points out that there are some differences between the IMS and the MRBI surveys relating to timing, sample sizes, differences in lower age limit, and the ways in which some areas were addressed in terms of the types of questions included in the MRBI survey that were not included in the earlier one. Nevertheless, there are many similarities between the two types of investigation. Hanley provides a good analysis of the most recent study.[26]

MRBI results show, even more so than those of the IMS, that the people of Ireland continue to place a high value upon the spiritual, despite the decline in religious practice. The European Values Survey in 1990 found that 85% of the Irish population got 'comfort and strength from religion' and an even higher number (98%) professed their belief in God. The most recent study reveals that 82% of the participants claimed that religion was either very important or fairly important in their lives. Even among the younger generation who have low rates of Church attendance, many value the importance of spirituality, with 65% of those aged 18–24 years indicating that it was important. Hanley concludes that 'there is a substantial majority of the Irish population, spread comparatively evenly across a generational cross-section, who consider themselves to be living lives which are in some way based on a relationship with God.' She goes on to say that when one considers the findings of both the IMS and the MRBI surveys, they show that Irish religious belief and practice are undergoing a profound change. 'It is important to keep in mind that beneath the surface of change and criticism there exists a strong spiritual core.' This appears to be an optimistic understanding of the challenge facing the Catholic Church in Ireland at the beginning of the twenty-first century. It seems more accurate to interpret the presence of, or desire for, a core spirituality as reflecting a postmodern attitude, especially among the young who are suspicious of, and reluctant participants in, religious institutions.

The results of the MRBI survey are less optimistic than those of the IMS study which was carried out approximately six months earlier. Weekly Mass attendance is down from an average of 66% to 60% for the country as a whole, although one has to keep in mind that there is, on average, a 3% margin of error in market research surveys of this type.

The principal reason cited by respondents in the MRBI survey who rarely or never attend Mass was that they found Mass dull or boring (27% in contrast to 18% in the IMS survey). A substantial segment in the MRBI poll also felt that priests were out of touch (23%) or that it was too much trouble to go to Mass. These figures are much higher than the equivalent results from the IMS research and demonstrate a growing indifference toward the most central sacrament of the Catholic Church. 'In short,' says Hanley,

> Both of the surveys conducted in the past year tell us that the outstanding feature of the devotional lives of almost all Irish men and women twenty-five years ago has become a low priority for an increasingly large percentage of the Irish population.[27]

Regarding the other outstanding feature of Irish Catholicism, regular participation in sacramental Confession, the results of the MRBI poll confirm those of the earlier IMS survey. Nearly half of the Catholic population (40%) claimed that they rarely or never took part in this sacrament, while only 1% said that they went to confession every two to three weeks. Although the questions were formulated differently in each survey, the combined results provide a picture of a sacrament in its present form going into what appears to be terminal decline. In the case of both surveys, the most telling point of comparison in measuring the decline of religious practice among Irish Catholics is to be made with the 1974 figures, which show that almost half the population (47%) attended sacramental Confession once a month or more frequently – five times the highest current figure.

Hanley points out that the implications of falling rates of Mass attendance and sacramental participation become clearer when the nature of the change is broken down by age and geographical distribution. Both surveys reveal that the principal differentiating factors for Mass attendance rates were age and area of residence. However, the more recent MRBI poll portrays a darker picture. It found that only 38% of the 18–24 year-olds attend Mass weekly (compared with 60% of the country as a whole) in contrast to the somewhat earlier IMS findings that showed that nearly half of those between 15 and 24 years attended Mass weekly. Part of the discrepancy here may be explained by the fact that the majority of 15–18 year-olds live with their parents.

Both surveys also confirmed that patterns of Mass attendance can be charted along an urban/rural divide. The IMS poll taken in the summer of 1997 showed that, on the whole, 83% of rural Catholics take part in the eucharistic celebration once a week or more often compared with 54% of urban dwellers. The MRBI January 1988 survey demonstrated a similar pattern, albeit with reduced attendance – 77% and 48%, respectively. The discrepancy between the urban and rural Mass attendance figures may be attributed to differing patterns of social life in rural and urban communities. Although it has diminished somewhat, there is still a fairly strong sense of community in rural Ireland in contrast to the atomistic character of the larger towns and cities. Another factor in the differing patterns of Mass attendance must surely be the fact that there is a greater concentration of young people in the urban centres, hence reducing the percentages.

The most significant contribution of the MRBI survey in January 1998 is that it investigated a social group who had hitherto not been studied as a unit, namely, the socially and economically deprived who live in urban areas. It had been estimated that Church affiliation among this group, as measured by Eucharistic and other sacramental participation was as low as 20% to 25%. In combining age and area of residence, MRBI produced the most dramatic results to date. Focusing on a suburb of a large city, which contains one of the highest concentrations of young, unemployed, and low wage earners in the country, data from the survey revealed that weekly Mass attendance in this area was only 7%. This has been described by the Catholic Bishops' Council for Research and Development as 'a shocking finding' when placed in the context of a national figure of 91% a little more than two decades earlier. On the basis of these statistics, it becomes clear that young people living in socially deprived urban areas no longer have any practical attachment to the Church and have virtually abandoned the weekly celebration of the Eucharist. In this regard, one concurs with the sentiments of John Elias that 'what the Church cannot afford is to be despised by the poor and small, by those who do not have another to help them.'[28] In the Judeo-Christian narrative, from Exodus to Calvary and beyond, Divine Presence finds a special home among the excluded and the oppressed.

There is something paradoxical in the fact that just as the Catholic Church, since the Second Vatican Council, has embarked on an increasing orientation toward the poor, oppressed, and socially deprived, these people have largely opted out of the Church in urban Ireland. Gregory Baum, Donal Dorr, and Dermot Lane are among the many commentators who have pointed to this new orientation of the Church that is not only reflected in political and liberation theologies, but also in the teaching of the Magisterium. Probably the most radical document issued by the Catholic Church to date was that which evolved from the Latin American bishops' meeting at Medellin in 1968 where, Dorr claims, they took 'the single most decisive step towards an option for the poor.'[29] Baum regards the declaration of the 1971 Synod of Bishops, entitled *Justice in the World*, as the turning point in the development of Catholic social teaching.[30] He claims that this development, which had its roots in Vatican II and the liberation movement in Latin American, has been fully endorsed by Pope John Paul II. An examination of his encyclicals and the various speeches that he delivers on his world travels reveal that John Paul not only affirms this new radical social orientation in the Church's teaching, but extends it significantly. Lane is of the same mind as Baum and Dorr regarding the Church's new self-understanding of her mission in the world. 'At this stage,' he says, 'it becomes possible to state that there has emerged within the official teaching of the Catholic Church a clear theological consensus concerning the integral relatedness of action for justice and the mission of the Church.'[31]

In briefly considering this new orientation of the Catholic Church, a credibility gap arises in that the most marginalized in Irish society do not perceive or experience the Church in the way it understands its own message and ministry. In this context, it is important to acknowledge that many of those who are without work or caught in a low-income cycle of poverty feel alienated from all institutions of society, as illustrated by the findings of the 1990 European Values Systems Survey. Nevertheless, while residents of marginalized urban areas may not have a particular antipathy toward the Church, it behoves a religious institution that claims to favour the socially and economically deprived to close the gap between what it believes and teaches and how this is perceived by its baptized members. In this regard, a major challenge faces the Catholic Church in Ireland at the beginning of the third millennium of Christianity.

When considering the causes underlying the changes in Irish religious practice among Catholics, particularly during the last decade, many commentators have speculated on a link between the 'scandals' faced by the Church and a growing sense of disillusionment or apathy among rank and file members. Hanley points out that this equation is not borne out – at least, not in any simple, direct correlation – by the two surveys being considered. While 73% of the Catholics consulted in the MRBI poll felt that these affairs had damaged the Church's authority to a substantial degree, an almost similar number of respondents (72%) in the IMS poll conducted on behalf of the Council for Research and Development claimed that their religious beliefs and practices had been completely unaffected by various revelations regarding clerical misbehaviour, which had become public since the beginning of the decade. It is clear that a majority of Irish Catholics perceive that the authority of their Church has been damaged, yet they refuse to allow this to interfere with their beliefs and religious practice. There is no new evidence, then, in the MRBI survey to affect the conclusion drawn from the earlier IMS study that the decline in active Church membership results from other than the sweeping socio-economic and cultural change that has affected the Republic of Ireland during the last two decades.

This cultural shift, which has seen the demise of traditional authoritarian society, is also reflected in people's readiness to question Church teaching on specific issues, particularly those of a social or moral nature. This was already evident in the results of the European Values Systems Survey in 1990, but has since accelerated. The MRBI poll revealed that only 30% of respondents reported that they agreed (either totally or somewhat) with the Catholic Church's teaching on divorce. Only 19% said that they agreed with the Church's position on artificial birth control, 21% agreed with priestly celibacy, and only 23% agreed with the Church's position on the ordination of women. This demonstrates a massive gap between the Church's teaching and authority and most members' beliefs on issues such as these.

In concluding this analysis of the two most recent national surveys regarding belief and practice among the Catholic population in Ireland, it may be clearly stated that Mass attendance has been declining more rapidly in the 1990s than in the previous two decades, particularly among the young, and there is nothing to suggest that this trend will not continue to accelerate. Moreover, both studies reveal with stark clarity the degree to which the young, especially those living in urban areas, have, within one generation, left behind a central feature of Catholic life that had endured for more than a century. Hanley sums up the situation by stating that

> The will to believe remains strong among all but the most chronically disaffectetd of Irish Catholics; however, the form which that belief will take is now undergoing a change more radical than any that has been witnessed since the last century.[32]

Northern Ireland

It has long been assumed that active Church affiliation among Catholics in Northern Ireland was very strong. This assumption was based on the minority status of Catholics and on the strained relations that exist between them and many of the state institutions in that part of the island. It was felt that religious observance would be more valued because allegiance to the Catholic Church had a greater symbolic value than in the Republic of Ireland. Even though the island of Ireland, with its two political jurisdictions, forms a single ecclesiastical entity, research into the beliefs and practice of Irish Catholics was confined to the Republic. The sparse evidence that is available for the North has been gleaned through European Values Systems Surveys. The lack of data on Northern Ireland made it difficult to compile evidence regarding Catholic belief and practice on the island as a whole. In order to paint a total Irish picture of Church commitment and also to test the popular hypothesis regarding Northern Catholics, the Bishops' Council for Research and Development commissioned Ulster Marketing Surveys (UMS) to conduct a survey comparable to that carried out in the Irish Republic investigating the effects of recent 'scandals' in the Church and to ascertain the religious behaviour and attitudes of Catholics in Northern Ireland. The survey, the most recent done on the island, took place in May 1998 and its findings contradict many deeply held assumptions.

Hanley points out that the most dramatic finding of the survey of Northern Ireland Catholics is that the rate of weekly Mass attendance, at 57%, is lower in Northern Ireland than in the Republic as a whole. There are also some significant differences in the profile of the North's Catholics who regularly participate in the Sunday Eucharist when compared to their Southern counterparts. In the Republic, only 50% of the population aged between 15–24 years attend weekly Mass. In the Northern jurisdiction, the figure for 16–24 year-olds is higher at 60%. There is, however, a decline in regular Mass attendance among Northern Catholics in the 25–34 year-old age group, of whom only 39% attend weekly Mass, whereas in this case the figure in the Republic is significantly higher at 51%. Table 7 shows the frequency of Mass attendance, according to age, among Northern Catholics.

For reasons that the UMS survey does not reveal, the youngest age group in Northern Ireland remains closer to the Church than their Southern counterparts, but among those in the second youngest bracket, there is a substantially higher rate of participation in the

Frequency of Going to Mass (Base: All Catholics)						
			Age			
	Total	16-24	25-34	35-49	40-64	65+
	346	77	84	94	48	42
	%	%	%	%	%	%
Daily	3	0	0	0	10	14
More than once a week	9	6	2	13	10	14
Once a week plus Holy Days	10	9	11	7	19	7
Once a week	35	45	26	31	33	44
Twice or three times a month	10	10	14	6	8	9
Once a month	10	5	10	2	4	2
About six times a year	5	4	2	4	0	2
2-3 times a year	3	5	4	4	2	2
About six times a year	4	4	2	4	0	2
Only rarely	6	5	4	4	2	2
Special Occasions only (eg. Christmas Easter)	7	5	11	10	0	2
Never	6	4	8	9	2	2
Don't know/ no reply	3	0	4	5	6	0

Table 7

Eucharist in the Republic. One suspects that this may be partly explained by the geographical size of the Northern jurisdiction where most university students, as well as the many young people who work in the large urban areas, return home each week-end, in which context there is still a certain family and social pressure to attend Sunday Mass.

Figure 5 compares weekly Mass attendance by age for Ireland North and South. Hanley draws attention to a caveat that needs to be entered when considering the comparisons.[33] When asked if they attended Mass two or three times a month (as opposed to weekly or more often), 10% of Northern Catholics claimed this to be the case, whereas the comparable figure among Southern Catholics was only 2%. Hence, if the weekly Mass attendance figure is added to the figure for those who attend two or three times a month, the combined figure for those who are attending two or more times a month or more often for Northern Ireland is 67%. This is comparable to the combined figure for the Republic which, according to the 1997 IMS survey, is 68%. If one accepts this figure rather than the figure of 60% resulting

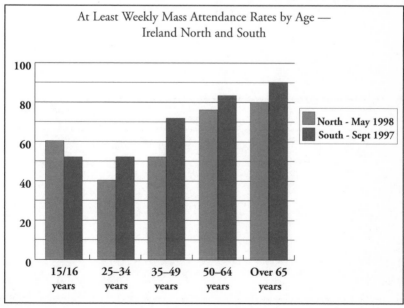

Figure 5

from the MRBI study in January 1998, it would suggest that levels of religious practice in the two parts of the island are, in fact, quite similar. Be that as it may, the UMS study has shattered the myth concerning the very high rate of Church allegiance among Catholics in Northern Ireland.

Table 8 shows the frequency of going to Mass now compared with three or four years ago. These statistics reveal that two-thirds of the respondents had a consistent attendance pattern compared to several years ago. However, 21% attended less regularly than before and only 10% had increased their attendance rates. Thus, overall attendance rates have decreased over time. The most telling statistics are that, among the general Catholic population, those who go less often to Mass today compared to three or four years ago are in the 16–24 age bracket (29%). This contrasts sharply with the group who are likely to be their parents (50–64 year-olds), only 2% of whom go to Mass less often today than a few years ago. The statistics for youth and young adults are ominous for the future of active Church affiliation.

Frequency of Going to Mass Now Compared to 3 or 4 years ago (Base: All Catholics)						
	Age					
	Total	16–24	25–34	35–49	40–64	65+
	346	77	84	94	48	43
	%	%	%	%	%	%
More often	10	9	15	6	13	7
The same/ no change	65	58	52	70	79	74
Less often	21	31	29	17	2	19
Don't know	4	1	4	6	6	0

Table 8

When participants in the Northern Ireland survey were asked to give reasons for going to Mass more often nowadays, UMS results revealed that a change in belief was the main reason for increased attendance, such as a more religious outlook on life (23%). A further 20% attended now for the sake of the family, or as their children had just started school (17%). When asked about their reasons for going to Mass less often nowadays, apathy and boredom were the main reasons given (26%). This was followed by pressure on time (15%) and other family commitments such as children (11%). 'Hypocrisy of the Church' (10%) and a sense of being 'old fashioned' and not aimed at young people (3%) were also off-putting to some respondents.

When these statistics are compared with those of the IMS survey it would appear that the rates of change in Mass-going habits are approximately comparable in the two parts of the island. The reasons offered by Catholics, both North and South, for changes to their patterns of participation in the Sunday Eucharist are also comparable. One category, however, that did emerge as unique in the UMS survey was the 6% who claimed they were attending Mass more often to pray for peace in the wake of the Good Friday Peace Accord. At the other end of the spectrum, the reasons given by those who claim to attend Mass less often today are also similar North and South. Hence, at the basic level of actual Mass-going habits, there appears to be little difference between Northern Catholics and their Southern counterparts.

The popular and long-held view that Northern Irish Catholics have a greater commitment to the Church than their Southern counterparts is not borne out by the Ulster Marketing Survey's findings. None of the Northern participants who were asked why they attended Mass more often made any reference to their position as Catholics vis-à-vis the state or its institutions. If it is the case that some Northern Catholics consider that their religion provides personal or community identity in their minority status, this does not seem to influence their participation in the Church's liturgy. Similarly, those who are participating in the Sunday Eucharist less often are doing so for reasons that relate to the changing cultural situation, as in the pressure of work or raising families, and a perception that the Church's sacred ritual and message is no longer relevant to their lives.

When the results of the UMS survey are examined with regard to
the other traditional hallmark of an Irish Catholic, that is, frequency
of sacramental Confession, a clear difference arises between North and
South. In the Northern jurisdiction, 19% made a monthly Confession
(or more often), in contrast to only 11% of Catholics in the South.
Furthermore, when asked if they never went to Confession, 19% of

	Frequency of Going to Confession (Base: All Catholics)					
			Age			
	Total	16–24	25–34	35–49	40–64	65+
	345	77	84	94	48	43
	%	%	%	%	%	%
Once a week	1	0	1	0	4	0
At least twice or three times a month	3	5	0	1	2	7
Once a month	15	8	11	11	27	35
About six times a year	8	9	4	12	13	5
2–3 times a year	21	29	15	16	21	26
Only rarely	22	26	23	26	15	12
Special occasions only (e.g., Christmas/Easter)	9	10	10	10	4	9
Never	19	13	33	22	6	7
Don't know/ no reply	3	0	4	3	8	0

Table 9

Northern Ireland Catholics said that this was the case, while the figure for the Republic was 25%.

Table 9 from the UMS study shows the frequency of participation in sacramental Confession according to age. It is noteworthy that the group with the lowest level of participation in sacramental Confession (25–34 year-olds) parallels that of Mass attendance. The higher than expected rate of attendance for the 16–24 age group may be due to parental influence and the provision of an opportunity for sacramental confession in the school setting. Consequently, it would be naive to interpret the percentages in the younger age bracket as reflecting an upturn in sacramental participation. While the figures for confessional practice among Northern Catholics are much higher than in the South, they still point to a major decline of attendance at this sacrament.

As mentioned earlier, one of the purposes behind the commissioning of the three recent surveys being discussed here (IMS, MRBI, and UMS) was to measure the extent to which the recent 'scandals' involving sexual abuse by clergy, which had swept the country, North and South, had affected religious belief and practice. The results of the Ulster Marketing Survey's poll showed that 23% did believe that recent scandals had affected their religious belief and practice to some extent. This was especially prevalent in the 25–49 year-old group, followed closely by the 16–24 age bracket. When asked in which way belief and practice have been affected, respondents said that lack of trust in clergy (33%) and lack of expectation of such behaviour (23%) were key ways in which they had been affected. It appears from the UMS results that the 'scandals' involving clerical sexual abuse did not significantly affect people's sacramental participation and it would be inaccurate to conclude that this accounts for the smaller numbers attending Mass and Confession.

Hanley points out that the most immediate obvious finding to emerge from the section of the UMS survey dealing with recent 'scandals' is, as is the case in other matters, 'the remarkable similarity of response North and South of the border.' In Northern Ireland, 69% of the respondents said that their religious belief and practice were completely unaffected by the recent unsavoury revelations, whereas the comparable figure in the IMS survey in the Republic is 72%.

Moreover, when respondents in both jurisdictions were asked to explain any ways in which their religious beliefs and practices had been affected by recent Church scandals, almost identical percentages – 33% in Northern Ireland and 34% in the Republic – spoke of losing trust in clergy and religious. What emerges from the UMS survey in the Northern jurisdiction is the same conclusion that arose from Hanley's analysis of the figures in the 1997 IMS study in the Republic: 'that most ordinary Catholics appear to be able to distinguish between the crimes of a small minority of clergy and religious, and the good work done by the vast majority.' When asked if their confidence in the local priests or bishops of their own diocese had been eroded by the recent 'scandals', only 16% (with regard to priests) and 14% (with regard to bishops) in Northern Ireland said that it had, whereas the figures in the Republic were higher at 29% for priests and 26% for bishops. 'This', according to Hanley, 'is one of the few statistics which supports the thesis that the Republic has become more secularized than Northern Ireland.'

When respondents were asked if they believed that the media's coverage of the 'scandals' had been fair, very similar proportions of respondents (45% in the North, 51% in the Republic) agreed that it had been fair. Moreover, the most frequently mentioned reason for believing that the media's treatment of clerical misbehaviour had been fair in both jurisdictions was the need to expose the truth (75% in the North, 63% in the South). Given the different patterns of media ownership and control in the two states, these latter findings, according to Hanley

> once again substantiate the idea that, in spite of obvious differences in the experiences of Catholics in the two parts of this island in relation to discrimination and social status, Irish Catholics, both North and South, relate to their Church in very similar ways.[34]

The UMS survey has, for the first time, provided detailed data that make it possible to compare religious belief and practice in the two jurisdictions that make up the island of Ireland. Thus, it is now possible to speak authoritatively of Irish Catholics, vis-à-vis their relations to the Church, as a single entity. The overwhelming conclusion that arises from the analysis of these data is that levels of religious practice, particularly as measured by Mass attendance, are declining and that the pace of this decline has accelerated during the last decade, particularly among the rising generation. The other clear conclusion that can be drawn from the analysis of the UMS data and its comparison with the data in the IMS and MRBI studies, is that the degree to which 'scandals' involving clergy and religious in recent years have influenced members of the Catholic Church is remarkably similar in the findings North and South. In both cases, the vast majority of respondents clearly differentiated between the deplorable actions of an anomalous few and the Church as a whole. On the basis of this distinction, it would seem that the majority of Catholics in the island as a whole have not let recent 'scandals' in the Church influence them in their religious practice, even if they are showing an increasing tendency to be critical of the Church and its clergy.

One is led to conclude that there are similar sets of cultural influences affecting religious belief and practice throughout the island of Ireland that go beyond the peculiar differences in the experience of living one's life as a Catholic north and south of the border, or indeed the actions of individual members of the clergy. In the words of Hanley:

> It may well be the case . . . that as Christianity enters its third millennium, the old political boundaries become increasingly permeable, and the lifeworlds of their citizens become increasingly subject to influences such as those of the electronic media which do not originate within the state.[35]

It seems to be an inescapable conclusion that the single most powerful influence on the beliefs, values, and attitudes of Irish Catholics, especially the young generation, is the rapid change in the lived culture on the island as a whole.

Notes

1. M. Drumm, 'A People Formed by Ritual', in *Faith and Culture in the Irish Context*, ed. E. G. Cassidy (Dublin: Veritas Publications, 1996), p. 83.
2. B. McCormack, *Perceptions of St Patrick in Eighteenth-Century Ireland* (Dublin: Four Courts Press, 2000), p. 51.
3. Drumm, op. cit., p. 86.
4. E. Larkin, *The Historical Dimensions of Irish Catholicism* (Washington, DC: Catholic University of America Press, 1984).
5. M. Bailey, *History and Conscience: Studies in Honour of Seán O'Riordan CSsR*, eds. R. Gallagher and B. McConvery, (Dublin: Gill and Macmillan, 1989), p. 275.
6. Larkin, op. cit., p. 77.
7. Drumm, op. cit., p. 95.
8. E. McDonagh, *Faith in Fragments* (Dublin, Columba Press, 1996).
9. E. G. Cassidy, introduction to *Faith and Culture in the Irish Context* (Dublin: Veritas Publications, 1996), p. 9.
10. C. T. Whelan and T. Fahy, 'Religious Change in Ireland 1981–1990', in *Faith and Culture in the Irish Context*, ed. E. G. Cassidy, (Dublin: Veritas, 1996), pp. 100-116.
11. Ibid., p. 15.
12. O. V. Brennan, *Report on Armagh Diocesan 'Listening Day'*. Unpublished manuscript (1996).
13. E. Doyle McCarthy, *Knowledge As Culture: The New Sociology of Knowledge* (London: Routledge, 1996), p. 107.
14. J. Dunne, 'Religion and Modernity: Reading the Signs' in *Faith and Culture in the Irish Context*, ed. E. G. Cassidy, (Dublin: Veritas, 1996), p. 118.
15. Cassidy, op. cit., p. 13.
16. A. Nic Ghiolla Phadraig, *Survey on Belief and Practice Among Irish Catholics* (Dublin: Research and Development Unit of the Irish Catholic Church, 1974).
17. A. Breslin and J. A. Weafer (Maynooth: Research and Development Unit of Irish Catholic Church, 1984).
18. M. MacGreil, *Prejudice in Ireland Revisited* (St Patrick's College, Maynooth: The Survey and Research Unit, Department of Social Studies, 1996), p. 170.

19. Whelan & Fahey, op. cit., p. 100.
20. C. T. Whelan, D. Hannon and S. Creighton, 'Unemployment, Poverty and Psychological Distress', *Journal of Social Policy* 22 (1991), pp. 141–172.
21. R. Breen and C. Whelan, *Social Class and Social Mobility in Ireland* (Dublin: Gill and Macmillan, 1996).
22. Whelan & Fahey, op. cit., p. 107.
23. D. Yankelovich, *The New Morality: A Profile of American Youth in the 1970s* (New York: McGraw-Hill, 1974), p. 9.
24. Whelan & Fahey op. cit., p. 114.
25. McDonagh, op. cit., p. 45.
26. A. Hanley, 'Attitudes to the Catholic Church: The RTÉ Prime Time/MRBI Survey' (Maynooth: Council for Research and Development, 1998 unpublished).
27. Ibid., p. 2.
28. J. L. Elias, *Studies in Theology and Education* (Malabar, FL: Robert & Krieger, 1986), p. 185.
29. D. Dorr, *Option for the Poor* (New York: Orbis Books, 1983), p. 257.
30. G. Baum, *Theology and Society* (New York: Paulist Press, 1987).
31. D. Lane, *Foundations for a Social Theology* (New York: Paulist Press, 1984), p. 118.
32. Hanley, op. cit., p. 6.
33. A. Hanley, 'Religious Confidence Survey', Northern Ireland (Unpublished report, 1998).
34. Ibid., p. 5.
35. Ibid., p. 6.

CHAPTER IV

THE BELIEFS AND VALUES OF FIVE IRISH YOUTH

In the previous two chapters, we have seen how contemporary Western culture, which is characterized by lingering modernity as well as by strong elements of post-modernity, has affected the beliefs, values, attitudes, behaviour, and Church affiliation of young people in general, with particular reference to those living in Ireland. Through the analysis of in-depth interviews with five different categories of Irish youth, this chapter sets out to illustrate in concrete terms the extent to which these young women and men have been influenced by a culture that has changed at a very rapid pace during their lifetime. The interview process endeavoured to enter into the varied life stories of these people with a view to eliciting descriptive data about their human, cultural, and religious experiences in the conviction that the meaning that one human being makes of his or her experience can shed significant light on a human or religious problem. A series of three interviews was conducted with each of the five participants. These have yielded rich data for fruitful analysis that illuminates the quantitative findings of the surveys examined in the previous chapter.

The three young women and two young men who were interviewed grew up in varied backgrounds and geographical areas in both the Northern and Southern jurisdictions that make up the island of Ireland. Sean and Fiona came from rural Ireland, the latter from a farm. Brigid spent her childhood and adolescence in rural Northern Ireland. Tara grew up in a suburb of Dublin city and Tom has lived most of his life in a socially deprived area of a large provincial Irish town. Sean is a committed member of the Catholic Church, just like his parents and grandparents. Fiona has a deep desire to be a committed member of the Church, but is extremely critical of the institution as it currently stands. Brigid has abandoned the faith of her parents and is now affiliated with a 'rainbow church'. Tara has a loose affiliation with the Catholic

Church and would not attend Mass or the sacraments on a regular basis. Tom no longer has any connection with institutional religion. Each of these young people grew up in homes where their parents were all committed to the Catholic Church in varying degrees.

Analysis of Interviews

An analysis of the five participants' stories reveals that these young Irish people are neither uniformly modern nor postmodern; rather, they embody significant elements of both, especially the latter. They do not consistently order their world in either a modern or postmodern way, nor may they even have the capacity for so doing. The modernist perspective is illustrated in a number of ways. Most of the participants have a high regard for the education system in Ireland, which is increasingly rational, scientific, and technological. They are not avid viewers of MTV; they can see its images as disjointed and one of them described it as 'ridiculous.' They value individualism, freedom from any kind of authoritarian structure, and being true to oneself – the constitutive ideal of modernity, according to Charles Taylor. Another feature of modernity, the atomism of the self-absorbed individual, is also evident at times. What Tom Beaudoin describes as postmodern youth's penchant for irony and parody is present but not strongly evident in the interviews.[1]

On the other hand, the human and religious experiences of most of these young people are shot through with many aspects of the culture of post-modernity. While they value the freedom of the individual, they reject the concept of the autonomous individual that is characteristic of modernism. In their search for community, whether of a small group of peers or a specifically religious community, most of them reject the premodern hierarchically structured concept of community in favor of the postmodern perspective, whereby a participant takes part as an equal and both influences and is influenced by that community. Moreover, this would be a sphere of healing and support. Some of these young people clearly reject religious hegemony and intolerance, and what Foucault describes as 'knowledge control' in faith commitment.[2] For them, knowing is embodied; truth is contextualized and experienced; it arises out of one's own experience of relating and reflecting. As one participant put it, the Church is so removed from what the spirit of life is meant to be about. It is so removed from real life, from experience . . . it holds itself back from the radicality of life . . . of real living, of real truth as something that is experienced.

The epistemological stance of these young people varied, but most of them seem to reject the epistemology of modernism, which holds that truth can exist apart from the knower. They favour diversity over absolutes, laud a plurality of viewpoints, and celebrate differences. They prize both community and individualism, but communities that are open to diversity are most appealing. This is reflected in Brigid's statement:

> I think it is important to recognize that we all have different needs and different ways of living and different ways of being, that we are all different, and that, provided we can live without damaging each other or damaging the earth, we need to have a lot of tolerance for each other.

She goes on to say that the only absolute wrong is hurting a child, especially sexually, but 'things that are wrong to me I would not say are necessarily absolutely wrong . . . I certainly would not judge somebody else, because it is part of their lifestyle.' Regarding the Catholic Church's teaching on sexual morality, she believes that the only absolute wrong is when someone violates somebody else, the precept of absolute wrong being: 'Do not take what is not freely given.' In coming to a decision as to what is right or wrong, Brigid would not be swayed by what any higher religious authority says or teaches. Instead, she would 'really look inside' herself and 'look to other people for their opinions, not to any religious authority.' This postmodern stance corresponds with that of the majority of participants who took part in the interviews.

Data from the interviews illustrate another dimension of postmodernity which has been referred to by many commentators, that is, the openness of this new sensibility to the mystical dimension of human and religious experience. The nature and extent of this penchant for the spiritual varies from person to person. Fiona's spirituality is nature-centered, God, and Christ-centered. When asked what gives most meaning to her life at present, she responded that her reason for wanting to live at all is the belief that her life, everybody's life, is a gift from God – the Creator God – and that the appreciation of a gift so graciously given should be passed on. She values 'every moment of life because it is an opportunity to live, to just be, to celebrate life and celebrate life with people around' her. She has a keen sense of the presence of God in nature, in the trees, the rivers, the flowers, the mountains, and in the very air she breathes. Yet, while God is 'the greatest force of love in the world,' and love is life, and this Spirit of love and life is everywhere, 'that Spirit of God is made personal, is made real and relational in Jesus, in human form.' This particular spirituality finds expression in a variety of prayer forms, ranging from drawing, writing, and experiencing nature to more structured meditation.

A somewhat different illustration of post-modernity's openness to mystery is exemplified in Brigid's spirituality. God is not always like a person. God is primarily a creative energy, a life-force that exists all around. She believes that there is a unity of all life-forces and that we 'are all very connected.' God is in the connection of all, 'of all that is life – all human life, animal and plant life, the air, the rivers – God is in absolutely everything around us.' Although this understanding of God is very impersonal, Brigid experiences God as very honest, true, kind, and patient. 'The God that I believe in,' she says, 'is very, very good and caring.' Prayer, which is largely unstructured, is a matter of giving thanks for animate and inanimate life as well as for the Life-force itself. Unlike Fiona's spirituality, this postmodern stance reflects a marked shift away from faith in a historically specific revelation, such as that articulated in the doctrine of the Incarnation and in the nature of God as expressed in the Trinity.

While Tara's spirituality differs from that of Brigid and Fiona, she too values the spiritual over the institutional Church in which she was nurtured. She describes herself as having 'great faith,' even though she does not go to Mass every Sunday and claims that 'you cannot judge somebody's religious beliefs or their faith by how often they got to Mass.' Her deep faith in a personal God is based on a more traditional spirituality that she inherited from her parents; it is faith in, and prayer to, a God who is always there to turn to in time of need. Tara feels that the Catholic Church should not be telling people to go to Mass every Sunday, that it is one's own choice, and that 'if you don't want to go, if you would rather talk to God wherever you feel you want to talk to Him, that is the way it should be.' This form of spirituality is not radically new but it does not need institutionalized faith for its viability and in this sense, bears the hallmark of a postmodern sensibility.

Tom's spirituality is not as explicit as that of the other participants in the research conversations. Nevertheless, even though he has abandoned any practical affiliation with the Catholic Church, he continues to search for a spirituality that is meaningful and sustaining. 'I have no doubt,' he says, 'that there is spiritual strength to be gained by your belief in something.' He believes in a higher power, 'that quiet knowing that there is something around.' Jesus Christ, while not the incarnation of God, was both a 'magical figure' and 'a very real figure, and that is lost in the Church's teachings.' In a typical reaction to modernity, he states that 'the body, mind, and soul are one.' Here again, one can taste the flavour of post-modernity as this young man's story reflects the evidence gathered from the quantitative surveys carried out in Ireland; young people may be abandoning organized religion but not faith in God or in some form of spiritual source.

Sean is committed to the Christian narrative as it is embodied in the doctrine, morality, liturgy, and prayer life of the Catholic Church. Although he grew up in a rural community that reflected more elements of premodernity than modernity, he stands firmly within the latter camp at present. He now works and lives in the city, but like the majority of people in rural Ireland, he continues to embrace the inherited Irish Catholic tradition in an increasingly secular culture. Sean grew up in a rural community that had a particularly strong community sense and he still prizes this enormously. His story is the only one that does not appear to reveal any elements of the culture of post-modernity.

Formation in a Catholic Culture

Four out of the five participants in the interview process were born into, and grew up in, homes that were characterized by a firm commitment to the Catholic Church. This was especially exemplified in weekly attendance at Mass and other Church devotions. While the fifth participant, Tom, may not have experienced an equally strong attachment to the Church, he did participate in the Sunday Eucharist each week with his parents during childhood and adolescence years. Furthermore, each of these young people attended Catholic schools for the duration of their primary and secondary school education. Data from the interviews are now examined in order to ascertain the influence of home, school, parish, and peers on these young people as they progressed through their childhood and adolescent years.

The Culture of Childhood

Most of those interviewed had a happy or very happy childhood at home and in school. Sean's father died when he was only nine years old, but this event served to bond the family together in care and support. Only one person had a rather unhappy childhood. Fiona was the youngest of four children in a traditional farming family. It was a quiet household and her parents were the type of people who were not able to express their emotions or feelings. She was always looking for acceptance and love but never experienced it. On the positive side, Fiona spent a lot of time outdoors and enjoyed the natural surroundings that provided free rein for her imagination.

In general, the childhood experience of these five young people was quite deeply religious. The Irish Catholic culture pervaded their homes, schools and parishes. This was unexpectedly the case, even in a Dublin city suburb. Tara describes her home as extremely happy and imbued with a religious atmosphere. 'Religion was very prevalent in it,' she says, 'and we were brought up to believe in everything that my parents believed in.' The family prayed together every night and morning. Sunday was the quiet day; they all went to Mass together in the morning and came home to the typical Sunday dinner. In the afternoon, the family went for a walk to the beach or to the mountains, but Sunday Mass was the central event in their lives. 'Of all the Sunday activities, the one thing that stands out in my memory as most important,' Tara says, 'was Sunday morning Mass.' Her parents grew up in rural Ireland and they both had a very strong religious commitment. Most of the people in the private residential estate where they lived came from the same background, mainly rural Ireland, and shared the same beliefs and values. For example, 'every Sunday morning at 11.30 a.m. there was a mass exodus to the Church'. While she did not have any sense of belonging to a parish community at primary school age, Tara did live in a neighbourhood with a strong sense of community, which is probably not typical of suburban Dublin. What stands out most about parish life in her childhood years was the presence of a particular priest. When he celebrated Mass 'he was real and made the Mass real and would talk to people afterwards.' She and her older brother really loved him and wanted him at their house all the time.

Tara spent eight very happy years at primary school and loved Sister X who was the Principal. The Catholic culture of the school reinforced the faith formation she received at home. Even though the school had a strong religious atmosphere and religion class lasted for nearly an hour each day, she does not now remember much about the content of the lessons. However, she can recall such things as taking part in a play based on the religion programme, First Communion and Confirmation preparation, and exploring the theme of family. There was communal prayer in the morning, before and after lunch, and prior to going home. Each classroom had a shrine to Mary and prayers were said to her each morning.

In Northern Ireland, the experience of a child who belonged to the Catholic community was very similar to that of a child in this Dublin suburb, except that there was an even stronger sense of Catholic identity. Brigid, who spent her childhood in a small town, had a more or less equivalent religious experience at home and at primary school to that of Tara. Family prayer was not quite as regular in Brigid's home but attendance at weekly Mass and all other Church devotions were woven into the tapestry of the local cultural experience. Brigid had only a slightly stronger sense of belonging to parish, which arose from meeting people outside Mass and taking part in a few events in the parish community centre. In both cases, belonging to parish essentially meant attendance at Sunday Mass and other religious services.

Not only was Brigid very happy at home, she also loved primary school. It was a convent school where the Catholic ethos was all-pervasive. 'We had a lot of fantastic nuns,' she says, 'so we did a lot of religious plays at school about different saints. We also had an assembly every morning with ten minutes of prayer.' There was prayer before lunch, after lunch, and throughout the day. A religion lesson was part of the curriculum each day as well. In a later interview, Brigid described the nun who was her school principal as one of the people who had greatest influence on her life, even though Brigid herself has now abandoned the Catholic Church.

The parish experience of the other three young people was fairly similar during their childhood years, with parish involvement being more or less confined to attendance at Church liturgies. Life at home varied from being very happy to being rather unhappy. Family prayer, in the form of the Rosary, was recited every evening in Fiona's home, and occasionally in Sean's household, whereas Tom did not experience any form of family prayer. In their respective primary schools, the religious atmosphere was not as all-pervasive as it was in Tara's or Brigid's experience, but the usual religion lessons were held, their memory of which is mainly confined to preparation for first Communion and Confirmation. Tom, who grew up in a socially deprived local authority housing estate, had a very negative experience of primary school and this was to have a lasting impact on his life. One teacher told his class that a lot of them would 'end up in the gutter' for the rest of their lives, a statement that he now has difficulty reconciling with the supposed ethos of a Catholic school.

The Culture of Adolescence
One of the surprising features of the five multiple interviews is the revelation that most of the participants were not heavily influenced by the then increasing secular culture of Ireland during their adolescent years. This is especially so in the case of a teenager living in a Dublin suburb during the last decade. Both she and her closest friends, who were her immediate neighbours, were largely untouched by the contemporary lived culture in that part of Ireland. This was due to the strong parental influence and the Catholic culture that pervaded their homes and private housing estate. However, on her own admission, this was not generally the case among her other peers in secondary school. Tara and her neighbourhood friends were not allowed out to discos and bars all during their time at secondary school, whereas

'everyone else in the school' was going out socially. According to her, these people were 'into the latest fashion and pop music (mainly American) and were taking alcohol and drugs.'

There was no significant change at parish level from childhood years. Neither Tara nor her friends were invited to take an active part in the liturgy or any other parish activity. The parents continued to adhere to the strict Sunday observance, but as their offspring gained the freedom, from mid-adolescence onward, to attend Mass with friends rather than family, strict adherence to the Sunday obligation diminished somewhat. Tara clearly remembers the first Sunday she did not go to Mass but went to a friend's house instead. Her thoughts were: 'Oh my God, my parents are going to kill me if they ever find out!' At sixteen years of age, she was keenly aware of a sacred obligation in her parents' culture. Since the priest she admired so much had already left the parish, Church life hardly influenced her at all from mid-adolescence onward.

The Catholic culture of a Northern Ireland teenager was not significantly different from that of the Dublin suburb. Brigid's family had moved from the small town of her childhood to a totally rural parish. The religious experience at home continued as before, with particular emphasis on weekly Mass attendance. This became more of a struggle from about the age of fifteen onward, and participation in the Eucharist was achieved through parental authority. One thing did help: a priest who was in residence in the new parish took a particular interest in young people and involved Brigid in a folk group that sang, not only in Church on special occasions, but also at various concerts over a wide area. This is the most pleasant Church-related memory of her adolescent years.

Despite her reluctance to attend Mass mid-way through her secondary school education, Brigid feels that the culture of Catholicism influenced her very much at that time. 'In terms of living in Northern Ireland,' she says,

> You identified strongly with your own religious community, with the people within your school. It was like every school was a different tribe and there wasn't a lot of interaction between the different schools, Protestant and Catholic.

This meant that there was little exposure 'to any school of thought other than the Catholic perspective.' Moreover, nearly everyone she knew was religious; 'nearly everyone went to Mass.' Nevertheless, despite the significant influence of a Catholic culture emanating from home, parish, and convent secondary school, 'a broader circle of people' began to make some impact on her ideas and values. A surprising finding here is that peer group influence was not a significant factor, except in the case of clothes. But 'social life had a huge impact . . . at that stage.' Brigid says that

> From one end of the week to the other, all you talked about with peers was where you were going at the weekend, and what you were doing the Saturday night before, what you had got up to, whether you had been drinking, if you had been with a fellow, or if you had been dancing all night.

In general, consumption of alcoholic beverages began at the age of 15–16 years for herself and the majority of her peers. One of the marked changes in the contemporary Irish cultural landscape is the dramatic rise in the numbers of adolescents consuming significant amounts of alcohol.

When one examines the conversations regarding the lives of the two rural dwellers in the Republic of Ireland, there are some surprising results. Throughout the years they spent at secondary school, neither Sean nor Fiona had any exposure to the new wave of disco-style youth entertainment that had swept the country during the previous decades. This means that they were largely unaffected by this aspect of foreign culture that had invaded the Irish landscape and, in many ways, their young lives were similar to those of their parents. Attendance at Mass and other Church devotions was unquestioned, as was the observance of traditional mores. While the move to a convent secondary school in the local town expanded Fiona's world, 'the main sphere of influence' was still her home. She kept a lot to herself, 'did not really go out, did not really take part in things.' Her clearest memory of adolescence is knowing what was on TV each day. She described her adolescence as 'the most depressing, uncertain and insecure time' of her life. This was especially true during the senior years at secondary school. 'I could not grow up,' she says, 'into my own kind of person as I hadn't the guts to oppose my parents. I always wanted their acceptance.' Fiona had a sense of guilt about everything since nothing was good enough for her mother. This was reinforced every time she went to Mass: 'I heard I had sinned, so that reinforced the guilt. That is one of the memories of Church: you sinned and, therefore, you are a bad person.'

Sean had an almost equally sheltered experience during the five years he spent at secondary school. For him, the primary influence in his life came from his mother and family, as well as the Christian Brother who was principal of his school. However, this was a happy time for him. He was very much involved in the local community and attended all Church liturgies, just as he had done during his childhood years. This was not typical of his age-group as he says: 'I was a lot more active in the Church at that stage of my life than many of the other students at secondary school.' In particular, he felt that his peers who lived in the town were exposed to, and influenced by, a different type of culture.

Tom's cultural experience during adolescence differed substantially from the other four participants. While he continued to attend Mass until the age of eighteen, the influence of the Catholic Church was quite limited. He did not experience a sense of belonging to his parish. Rather, he identified more with the local youth club and was 'influenced very much by a youth leader in the area who had a very liberal and open-minded way of looking at things.' In contrast to the other young people who were interviewed, Tom continued to have a very negative experience of the education system. As a result, he left secondary school after three years at the invitation of the Brother who was principal. After a failed attempt at a vocational training programme, he was accepted back into his former secondary school where he completed second-level education. The only bright light on an otherwise dark educational horizon was religion class in secondary school because, according to Tom, it was 'one of the only classes where you were respected as an individual.'

Tom appears to have been much more heavily influenced by popular culture during his adolescent years than the other young people who were interviewed. He was influenced by 'music, bands, films, TV, magazines, and books.' He was 'drinking in everything at the time,' watched MTV, and felt that the lyrics in the songs were rightly criticizing the adult world and its authority figures. He described this world of song and music as 'a safe place to go because I thought I was not thinking like mainstream society; it was an alternative way of thinking, a safe place.' His first introduction to this 'new kind of culture' came at twelve years of age and had an increasing influence on him thereafter. Now in his twenties, Tom acknowledges that one's ideas, values and overall attitude to life are affected by the type of culture to which one is exposed. This corresponds with Sean's perception of cultural influence from a rural angle.

Tom was the only one of these five young people who had a significant religious experience outside of his local parish. At the age of sixteen, he was taken on a youth pilgrimage to Medjugorje where Our Lady is reputed to have appeared to a number of young people. He went with an open mind, even though he did not have much faith in apparitions. He had 'a very deep religious experience of sorts' there and it awakened him to his own spirituality. This, however, was unrelated to the reported visions and did not have a lasting effect on him. Upon returning home, he joined one of the prayer groups that were formed as a result of the pilgrimage. However, this was rather short-lived as he got 'really turned off' by the 'fundamentalist, traditional Catholic teaching – the devil is everywhere; sin, darkness; the revelations – associated with the Medjugorje prayer groups.' This reaction might serve as a warning to Church leaders and to those in youth ministry who might be tempted to turn back the religious and spiritual clock, thereby losing ideal opportunities to respond to the spiritual openness of the rising postmodern generation.

Exposure to a Broader Culture
One of the unexpected findings arising out of the in-depth conversations with five different types of Irish youth was the knowledge that all of them were in some way involved in the Catholic Church, at least by taking part in the Eucharist each weekend up to the age of eighteen years. This was primarily due to the influence of their parents and the general Catholic culture of their local areas. It was not until they left home to attend college or enter the workforce

that this affiliation to Church was challenged. When the culture of family and immediate neighbourhood, which was characterized by a strong attachment to the Church, clashed with the wider culture of university and city, the culture of childhood and adolescence was severely challenged. The knowledge gained from these five interviews reflects the pattern of Church attendance among young people which is revealed in the most recent surveys that have been undertaken both in Northern Ireland and the Republic of Ireland: disaffiliation from the Church tends to accelerate in late adolescence, particularly among those who move away from home.

The Culture of Tertiary Education and the World of Work

As an adolescent, Tara was largely unaffected by the new culture that was sweeping Ireland. Peer influence was confined to a small group of friends who lived in the neighbourhood. While other girls at school told them about being out to discos and bars at the weekend, 'taking alcohol and drugs and generally having a good time,' this did not really affect them as they 'lived in a different world.' In her own words, 'looking back on it we didn't have a clue.' At this stage of her life, the strongest influence still came from her parents. She recognizes this as unusual, since most girls in the school 'were heavily influenced by what went on in the world around them – TV, videos, music, fashion, alcohol, and drugs.' Because she and her group of friends were not taking part in the contemporary social youth culture they did not have contact with the majority of girls in secondary school outside of class time. These had much more freedom than Tara and her friends, as their parents were from the Dublin area. She goes on to state that: 'I think people from rural Ireland have very different values and beliefs than people in big cities; it is like two different cultures.'

It is not surprising, then, that entry into nursing school in one of the largest teaching hospitals in Ireland came as 'a big culture shock' for Tara. It was her first time living away from home and she began to experience life 'in a new, liberated way.' She was out in bars every night of the week and even though she was not imbibing alcohol (which nobody could believe), it was great to be seeing what she had not seen in her life up to now. She and her new friends 'had such a fabulous and exciting time'. She says that, 'When I moved away from home, my values and opinions changed because I was exposed to a different type of culture. During this period, I gradually drifted away from the Church and attendance at Mass became less frequent.'

Brigid reported that the thought of not having a religion would not even have occurred to her before leaving home in Northern Ireland, since everyone there belonged to some Christian Church. It was only when she went to college in Dublin and was exposed to a new religio-cultural world that her life took a turn that eventually led to her abandonment of the Catholic faith. She had some friends there who were extremely conservative Catholics, others who did not consider themselves Catholic at all, and still others who felt more aligned with the Buddhist tradition. Her friends had 'so many diverse opinions about things' that it led her more and more to seek out her own answers. Commenting on her experience at the university where she studied law, Brigid states:

> I would have been exposed to different ways of thinking. I was thrown into a more pluralistic type of culture than the one I grew up in, and I really had to look at some of the beliefs that I had taken for granted and re-assess those from the ground up and see how solid they were, and see what suppositions they just made.

She began to feel that there were certain values espoused by the Catholic Church that 'enabled people to judge other people in a negative light, for example, gay people.' In particular, the 'ritual of Mass' no longer had any really special place in her life, even though she occasionally attended a folk Mass in Dublin city, which had very good music and was presided over by a very broad-minded priest. During any weekend that was spent at home, Brigid went to Mass in order to 'appease' her parents. This pattern, which reflects the practice of nearly all those who were interviewed, may account for the survey results that consistently show a higher percentage of young people taking part in Mass prior to twenty-one years of age than afterwards. As is the case with most young people who go to college or enter the workforce away from home, Brigid's links with her native parish became more and more tenuous.

Brigid's life was totally untouched by the university chaplaincy or any form of pastoral care during college years. Apart from peers, the most significant influence came from one of her professors who 'really spoke the truth' and was 'very down-to-earth.' He played an active part in one of the college societies, the Irish Council for Civil Liberties, of which Brigid was a member. Meetings of this society discussed controversial issues such as gay rights, divorce, and abortion and took a liberal stance in regard to them. She also did a project in the human rights class on how transsexuals were legally gender identified, as opposed to how they were medically gender identified in the different countries of Europe. With increasing exposure to a culture that appreciated diversity and challenged traditional moral positions, Brigid questioned many of the values inherited during childhood and adolescence. 'At that stage,' she comments, 'I really felt that the Catholic Church was not for me anymore.'

Interestingly enough, it was a priest, Brigid's uncle, who unintentionally contributed to her decision to part ways with the Catholic Church. While she would have felt that there are definitely many things about the Catholic religion that are very valuable, 'the whole parcel' did not appeal to her anymore. She wanted to choose what she liked about the Catholic religion and still call herself a Catholic, while rejecting 'so many aspects' that she did not feel were 'morally okay.' Her uncle, however, who 'is very hard core and a very ultra-conservative Catholic,' was very insistent that she could not pick and choose what part of the Catholic religion was for her. After many arguments with him about this, she said: 'Then in that case I reject it all.' She goes on to say:

> I did not want to reject it all because I liked many aspects of it . . . but for him that was not okay. You had to take all or nothing. . . . His attitude was not a bit helpful. If he had been more open, it would have been much better for me, absolutely.

It is ironic that in dissociating herself from the Church, Brigid no longer took part in her favourite liturgical experience, the Easter Vigil, which is at the heart of individual and community spirituality in the Catholic Church.

Among those who were interviewed, Fiona was the one who least entered into popular culture during the five years she spent at secondary school. She was also the only one who went on to study theology at university level. At the age of seventeen, this was the first time she was ever away from home, and meeting 'just so many different people with so many different attitudes.' College was a place where her mind 'just grew' and where she 'came to understand so many things' and 'think so much about life as well.' She developed both intellectually and in her ability to relate to people. Fiona loved the study of theology. It was a wonderful intellectual challenge but gave no spiritual satisfaction. All of her initial friends studied theology and were very much into attending Mass, even on a daily basis, and she did likewise. Initially, then, her ambient culture at college was not typical of the popular culture that characterizes university life in Ireland. However, it was only a matter of time before she 'went through a period of revolt' and raised the question: 'Is God really around?' She still went to Mass, though less often, but it was experienced as dead and boring, attendance being out of a sense of duty rather than desire.

Not only did Fiona find Mass 'totally uninspiring,' she also discontinued her regular visits to the college chapel for quiet space and private prayer/meditation. However, after a relatively short lapse of time, she realized that she needed to have her 'own little prayer life' and this developed as she pursued theological studies and post-graduate work in the secular domain. Developing a prayer-life became increasingly important at postgraduate level, since this was the first time in her life that she was 'not directly connected to anything religious.' She comments:

> I really had to make an effort because I wasn't surrounded by the religion at home, and I was not studying religion, and it was then I really had to decide . . . and I thought that when I was praying and when I was connected to Jesus in some way things were going okay.

Ironically, the more she became 'spiritually alive,' the less she appreciated the Mass, 'the less the Mass became important'; gradually she 'just got frustrated' and ended up not always going, even on Sundays. This appears to reflect a postmodern sensibility, where the spiritual search becomes more important than participating in Church-related religious activity. Fiona's reaction to the experience of religion at home, which had not changed since her childhood and adolescent years, paralleled this. It still consisted of going to Mass and saying the rosary. These were both experienced as 'boring and deadening' and she gained more, spiritually, by going for a walk through the fields – the 'best place of prayer.'

It is noteworthy that just as was the case with Brigid, the university chaplaincy did not touch Fiona's life. However, one member of staff who was a priest did take time to listen to her and provided the space to tell her story. She describes this as a form of religious experience:

> At last I found somebody who cared enough to listen to me and my story. It was my first real experience of someone giving unselfishly. The many hours I spent in his presence turned into a sort of religious experience because that is what I had seen Jesus as – a person who was willing to give and provide space.

Already exposed to popular culture during his adolescent years, Tom eventually completed secondary education and entered a regional technical college where he spent three years. It was during this period that he lost contact with the Catholic Church. Once again, the chaplaincy personnel had no impact on his life. He says that, 'It was not really a conscious decision to pack in the Church; it just happened.' He stopped attending Mass and gradually lost all contact with the faith community into which he was baptized and catechized. The only religious experience that Tom had during college years involved a visit to a Protestant church and service with a female friend who belonged to that faith community. He found this to be meaningful and described it as 'a very real ceremony.' It was a small inclusive congregation with a high level of participation, and this appealed to him very much, in contrast to a cathedral Mass which is 'nice to see.' The one kind of liturgy that seems to appeal to contemporary youth is that which involves a small community. Brigid and Fiona also referred to their desire to be part of an intimate faith community. Many commentators and religious educators today regard this as a postmodern sensibility. Tom describes the Catholic Church as 'all pious and proper and sterile and clinical and detached.' During the years he attended Mass there was always 'a sacred space between you and the priest, that is always communicated'. The only Masses that he enjoyed and found meaningful were those celebrated in someone's house with a small group of people. On those occasions, the sacred space did not exist; rather, one became 'part of that sacred space' and 'the breaking of bread was a genuine breaking of bread.'

During his years at college Tom was exposed, by way of reading, to Eastern religions. He liked the 'whole train of thought there--body, mind, and soul incorporated.' This again appears as a reaction to the culture of modernity that created divisions between the cognitive and affective dimensions of the human being. As a result of his exposure to the Eastern way of thought, Tom concluded that 'There is not just any one avenue to God.' There are many avenues, and 'Catholics do not have the copyright on the whole thing.' This challenge to the metanarrative in favour of many grand narratives is a mark of post-modernity; not only is the notion of disembodied absolute truth rejected, but also faith in any one way of explaining the meaning of human existence.

During his adolescent years, Sean was 'much more influenced by the local culture of the parish' than he was by 'the wider culture, the current fast-paced culture in Ireland.' He was still answerable to his mother and also to his uncle, from whom he learned much. After completing secondary education he enrolled in a pre-employment class because of the influence of one of the teachers in the Christian Brothers' school that he had attended. As a result of this he very quickly entered the workforce and became very happy in his first job, which involved travelling on behalf of a company throughout Ireland. Despite this exposure to a new way of life where he 'got to see plenty' and 'met a lot of different people,' Sean continued to be very involved in his native parish community. He says: 'My thoughts never changed about it and I tried to be as active as possible.' Among the five young people who were interviewed, Sean is unique in this regard. He is also the only one who was 'still going to Church every Sunday' and occasionally to devotions. Despite this, he is clearly disappointed at never having been asked to play an active part in the liturgy or other specifically religious events in the parish. 'The one thing' he did notice was that 'you were eighteen or nineteen years of age and nobody reached out to you and said you were responsible or whatever.'

Sean now works in a large city and is ambitious to progress in the modern world, but he still cherishes the values of his family, Church, and local community. He recognizes that contemporary Irish culture does affect him but not to the extent that it affects most people with whom he is in contact. He says that 'life has changed in Ireland in the '90s, even compared with the '80s' but he can balance the values that he has inherited from Church, family, and local community with the values of the culture in which he is now immersed. He can 'juggle the two of them,' but puts more emphasis on inherited values than most other people of his age. He comments: 'You still have contact with your family and you still hold the family values that you were brought up with, taught, and learned.'

Sean's story appears to illustrate the findings of surveys on belief and practice that have been carried out in Ireland over the last few decades. Results from even the most recent studies show that affiliation with the Catholic Church, especially as exemplified through Mass attendance, continues to be strong in rural Ireland. His own impression about the rapidly increasing pace of change in the last decade is also borne out in the findings emanating from quantitative research. He notes the lack of respect for authority as a particular result of the rapidly changing economic and social environment and observes that: 'When I was a kid you would look up to and respect your elders and respect people in places, but there are kids at a young age now and they do not have the same respect within them that was the case a few years ago.' This reflects what commentators on post-modernity describe as 'a levelling of hierarchies.' The other trait of postmodernism to which Sean refers is the lack of respect for absolutes which is characteristic of contemporary Irish youth:

> It used to be that you listened to and respected the issue. . . . If somebody had something to say, you did not knock the person down . . . whereas now, young people have a more 'I am right and you are wrong' kind of attitude. Each person decides what

is right and what is wrong, without any regard for the point of view of any human or religious authority.

The Impact of Religious Education at Primary and Secondary School

Only one of the young people who were interviewed reported that he had a negative experience of education at primary level. This did not apply to religious education, his memory of which centres around First Confession, First Communion, and Confirmation. While he is rather cynical regarding the preparation for and participation in these sacraments, catechesis on the Holy Spirit does seem to have had a positive effect. In mid-adolescence it aided him in formulating belief in God and to this day he has a belief in the Holy Spirit. One wonders about the quality of pre-sacramental religious education upon hearing the comment: 'I remember my first confession, coming down the Church hill that day and thinking: Jesus, this is great . . . new man now . . . no sin on my soul . . . if I get killed now I will go to heaven straight away.' There is no mention of 'sin' or 'soul' in the relevant religious education programme, so perhaps this inappropriate language for a six- or seven-year-old was introduced by parents or by a particular teacher or priest.

Religious education at primary school had a somewhat neutral effect on two of the other four who were interviewed with the exception of one class when, after the death of one of the girls' parents, the schoolmaster had a discussion with them 'about the meaning of death and why death happens.' Fiona comments: 'I listened because it meant something to me . . . he was telling us what he thought; it was not a rhyme; it was a real thing and it seemed to make sense.' The two participants who have been most influenced by their religious formation at primary school are Tara and Brigid. They both went to convent schools where there was 'a lot of emphasis on religion.' They had religion books and religion class each day, but the lasting impact came from particular teachers, especially nuns, and the all-pervasive religious atmosphere in the school.

A review of the transcripts from the fifteen interviews reveals that religious education at secondary level was largely ineffective for the five young people who participated in this study. As Fiona said, 'I remember more of primary school religious education.' None of the five had negative memories of religious education at this level; rather, it appears to have had a neutralizing effect. Two people spoke about the positive experience they had in the religion class, particularly at senior level, where much of the content had a social orientation. It was described as somewhat akin to a civics class that had an open forum with lots of time to discuss topical issues. Fiona remembers it as a time when there were 'opportunities to question things, question life and question choices, and question who we were and what our conscience was,' whereas Tom remembers it as an opportunity to discuss 'the present state of religion in Ireland' as well as to learn about other world religions such as Hinduism and Islam. For the most part, the other three participants have only a vague recollection of what was taught or discussed in the religious education class, one criticism being that 'There are certain issues that could have been discussed better . . . like sex,' the things that were talked about among peers.

There is a general feeling in Ireland at the present time that religious education at secondary school level is largely ineffective and may even be in a state of crisis. This is a widespread view among parents, church leaders, and religious educators themselves. It is noteworthy that none of the five young people who were interviewed for this study made any reference to the Christian language of story, doctrine, liturgy, or morality when discussing the religious education that they participated in at secondary school. While these young people are searching for mystery and spirituality, they appear not to be literate in the languages of faith as an authentic aid to this search for ultimate meaning. Kevin Nichols believes that 'learning the languages of faith is an indispensable task'.[3] Ideally, the language of narrative, doctrine, liturgy, and morality should interact and nourish each other. But this requires a form of religious education that will enable young people to clearly understand and fluently speak the four primary languages of the Christian tradition. Indeed, the predicament of the religious education enterprise is not peculiar to Ireland. Beaudoin notes that religious illiteracy is a hallmark of postmodern youth.[4]

Considering that the Catholic Church since the Second Vatican Council has embarked on an increasing orientation toward the poor, oppressed and socially deprived, it is surprising that none of the five young people who were interviewed had any awareness of this. This new orientation of the Church, which is not only reflected in political and liberation theologies but also in the teaching of the Magisterium, has been increasingly emphasized during the second half of the last century, but it did not surface in any of the conversations about religious education in secondary school. It appears that it is either not sufficiently emphasized in the texts being used or it is not focused on by the religious educators. As Tom put it: 'I don't think it was done with that much passion, because if it was done with passion, I would remember it.' When pressed on the issue of the social dimension of the Christian message, Brigid replied: 'We were certainly never taught to condemn people for being in poverty, which is an attitude a lot of kids have.' Teachers 'would never have referred to particular Church documents' but there was a general message given about the importance of caring for the poor.

In contrast to secondary school, the importance of caring for the poor received a lot of emphasis at primary level, even if this was mainly focused on the poor of the developing countries. In one primary school, 'Hardly a day went by that caring for the poor was not talked about'; returning African missionaries visited schools and talked about 'how poor the children were over there.' What one person described as 'this message of love' that was taught in religious education classes left a lasting impression and affected attitudes and behaviour to this day. While it is not appropriate to treat official Church documents at this level, and while the emphasis given to the social dimension of the Christian message is praiseworthy, it is a weakness of the current approach to religious education at primary and secondary levels that children and young people are not made aware of the official Church stance vis-à-vis the poor and socially deprived.

Commentators on the influence of popular culture on young people's values and attitudes point to the importance of cultural discernment or cultural critique. During the interviews with the five young people, searching questions were asked in an effort to ascertain to what extent their secondary school educational experience encouraged or empowered them to critique contemporary culture, or at least to 'offer some critical distance from which to view culture.'[5] Each of the five participants reported that no significant attempt was

made, even in the religious education classes, to examine the processes
that form individuals and society, to critique popular culture from a
Christian perspective, or to analyse cultural production and the
formative influence of culture on people's lives. One school made
some attempt to deal with this issue by allotting one hour per week for
'social something', but 'the teacher hardly ever showed up,' thereby
indicating the lack of importance that was attached to this subject in
the overall school curriculum. The little help that students did receive
in this area came through the study of history and English. Fiona
reported that while nothing was done in religious education classes,
English literature and history did help. The particular teacher that she
had for both subjects did not view education as 'something you had to
do just to get exams.' He always asked them 'to think about things and
never take anything for granted.' He taught them 'to look very much
into culture, to look very much into the way that people live and how
that changes.' Those who were interviewed generally expressed
disappointment about the lack of help that they were given to deal
with issues of popular culture, such as the sexual revolution, which was
even then affecting their lives.

The Image of the Catholic Church

The attempt to gain an understanding of how five young Irish people
perceive the Church yielded very negative results with one exception.
Sean, the only one who is still faithful to the Sunday obligation and to
the Church's moral laws, has a high regard for the Catholic Church
and rates it among the best institutions in the country. The reaction
among the other four varied between very critical and somewhat
critical. When she heard the word 'church', Brigid said that the first
image that comes to mind is that of 'an institution that is concerned
about preserving itself at all costs. It is not a flexible institution. It is a
rigid institution with a rigid set of values.' She is of the opinion that
preservation of the institution is more important to the hierarchy than
preservation of the values that it is supposed to espouse. As an example
of this, she cites the official Church reaction to the accusations of child
sexual abuse by priests, and she claims that the bishops, in these
instances, were more concerned with the image of the Church and of
the priesthood than they were with the protection of innocent

children. She does acknowledge, however, that many individuals within the Catholic Church are not like that. 'Many priests,' she says, 'are absolutely great, very broadminded . . . would care about what is really important,' but 'their hands are tied by the institution. They are not able to express themselves in a way that they would like to', and, in an interesting perception, she says that 'they are not able to live their lives in a way that is compatible with their own moral genesis, their own moral rightness.' Brigid sums up her attitude in a typical postmodern comment: 'I would be suspicious or critical of the institutional Church.'

The severity of this Church criticism was entirely unexpected from a young person who is working full time in a youth retreat centre in between graduate and postgraduate studies. The image that Fiona uses for the Church is that of a prison-like building: 'It has got chains, it just holds you down, it is restrictive, and anything negative I can think of.' Instead of being a community of people where one experiences care and intimacy, equality and democracy, the Church is a 'cold and anonymous' institution. Reflecting a clearly postmodern sensibility, Fiona views the Church as a block to the search for 'real faith' and genuine spirituality and as the antithesis of genuine Christian community where hierarchies are levelled.

Not surprisingly, Tom is as suspicious of, and negative towards, the Church as he is towards institutions in the country generally. 'What is the Church,' he asks, 'because the Church to me is non-existent.' He feels that the Church needs a good public relations person who could tell people 'what it is about.' His position seems to be typical of those who live in socially deprived urban areas, 93 per cent of whom, according to a most recent survey, no longer have any practical attachment to the Church. Tara's attitude toward the Church is rather neutral. Even though she does not join in the celebration of the Eucharist regularly, she could not see herself 'wanting to move away from the Catholic Church, at this stage anyway.' A loose affiliation with the Church is important to her, and in this regard, her attitude reflects that which is revealed in recent quantitative research in Ireland. Indeed, her attitude may not be as indifferent as that of the average young person who has stopped attending Church. She has sufficient interest to call on the Church to be 'more open-minded about young people' and about the younger generation's attitudes and values, since they and their children are going to be the future of the Church if it is to have a future at all.

The Influence of Church Teaching

Surveys on belief and practice among Irish Catholics during the last few decades have shown a sharp decline in adherence to Church teaching and to what Whelan and Fahey refer to as 'the virtual abandonment by many Catholics of tenets of their religion having to do with reproductive and sexual morality'.[6] The most recent studies indicate that only a minority agree with the Church's position on divorce, birth control, celibacy, and the ordination of women. The in-depth conversations with five members of the rising generation illustrate this *par excellence*. The only exception, for most of them, is divorce, but one suspects that this may have more to do with their youthful idealism than it has with adherence to Church teaching.

Each of the young people who were interviewed acknowledged that some of the teachings of the Catholic Church do have an influence on their attitudes and behaviour, albeit implicitly or indirectly. Brigid, who is most alienated from the Church, believes that 'a lot of the teachings of Christianity are great,' for example, 'loving your neighbour and taking care of people.' But the Catholic Church goes too far when it enters into the specifics of people's lives, 'when it begins to condemn people for what they do.' She thinks that the Church should not interfere in 'the sex lives of married couples and in celibacy for priests.' People should be given a lot of freedom in regard to how they live their lives, particularly in the area of sexuality. Brigid has not agreed with the Church's teaching on premarital sex since mid-adolescence and feels that 'if you loved someone enough' it is only right to express that love sexually and not wait until after marriage. In general, she acknowledges that exposure to the Catholic Church throughout childhood and adolescence probably has had an influence on her life. While she does not feel that it influences her values at the moment, she states: 'It is hard to tell how much of my make-up comes from growing up in the Church.'

All those who were interviewed believe that the majority of their generation do not agree with, or observe, the Church's teaching in the area of sexual morality. Sean is the only one who observes it, but while he agrees with nearly all of Catholic teaching, this is the one area where he would question the Church's position. This is indeed significant and reflects the impact of the sexual revolution in contemporary culture on even the most committed young Catholic. Tara says that this is 'not a bad reflection on the youth' and that the best way to deal with the Church's teaching on this issue is to 'pretend you do not know about it.' Tom reported that because he is living with his girlfriend there is 'some guilt in operation.' He blames 'Catholic pigeon-holed people' for this, and says that he is trying to 'work away from guilt,' since it is a 'useless emotion.' Since he loves his girlfriend, he feels that what he is doing is right and, in any case, he states: 'Don't let a crumbling, moralistic Church dictate to me how to live my life when their own shop is not in order.'

The three young women disagree with the Catholic Church's teaching regarding the ordination of women. Brigid and Fiona, in particular, consider it to be a grave injustice. Fiona feels that it is 'hard to be a woman in the Church.' Recently, she looked at a friend who was just ordained and was very envious of him, not of his position, but of the fact that she felt called to that same role in the Church. 'It is frustrating,' she said, 'watching people murder ritual, murder liturgy and Eucharist, and offer people dead words, when you know there is so much life you could give that.' In general, Fiona finds the teachings of the Catholic Church to be helpful. They are a 'fixed mark' or 'reference point' out of which she has grown, and against which she can bounce her own ideas. They are the only boundaries she has that come from outside herself, and these teachings are the values she will challenge on her faith journey. 'When I try to make decisions on how to live my life,' she says, 'it is those values that I do challenge and choose to either accept or reject.' These teachings, however, must never be imposed. They are 'like minefields of rules and regulations,' quite like those of the Pharisees who had a rule for almost everything under the sun. It is difficult to come to a clear conclusion as to whether Fiona's stance is modernist or postmodernist in this particular area. On the one hand, she appears to be accepting foundational principles, even if they are there to be challenged, but on the other hand, she goes on to say that the only absolute is God's love. This is the essence of living or the essence of the truth: 'God's love is present to all people unconditionally and God's forgiveness is there for all people unconditionally.' This appears to be an anti-foundational position and it is probably safe to conclude that Fiona is leaning toward the postmodern perspective in this, as in other areas of her life.

Primary Influences on Beliefs and Values

It is clear that, with one exception, the primary influences on the beliefs, values, attitudes, and behaviour of the young people who were interviewed no longer come from the Catholic Church, as was the case with all of their parents. Nevertheless, the conversations revealed that parental influence still had an extraordinary impact on the lives of these young people. Each would acknowledge, in varying degrees, that the values that were inherited from parents have made a lasting impression. When one considers that until a generation ago the influence of the Catholic Church permeated Irish society, it is not surprising that a residue of Catholic belief and practice, as well as an openness to the spiritual dimension of life, is an inherent part of these young lives.

Each of the five participants in this study spoke about the powerful influence of their parents and home environment during childhood and adolescent years up to the age of eighteen. In some cases the language used demonstrated how profound this influence was. Tara's parents 'definitely had a big influence' and 'still have a big influence' on her outlook on life. Not surprisingly, Sean's mother, brothers, sisters, and uncle had 'the biggest impact' on his life. Even Brigid, who has turned her back on the type of religious commitment that is central in her parents' lives, claims that they are the people who have exerted 'the biggest influence' on her overall attitude to life, 'definitely my parents,' she says. Looking back over her life to date, Fiona feels that her parents' 'sense of duty, their sense of doing things right,' and the religious setting of the home where she 'always did have something of a sense of Jesus and of the presence of God' have left a lasting impression. While she describes her mother's influence as 'a very negative one,' it still affected her as a person and gave her a sense of responsibility. Tom, who grew up in 'the latter end of a Catholic society,' also acknowledged that the foremost influence on his life came from home, especially his father. He came from 'a traditional working-class urban family' and learned in this environment the importance of treating people with respect, especially the socially deprived.

According to these young people, there is a clear correlation between care and influence. It appears that the people who care most for the rising generation have the greatest influence on them. Tom states that 'There is a connection between care and influence, most definitely.' Apart from his family, he was most influenced by a nun who came to live in the government-sponsored housing estate and also by a youth leader who was very anti-institutional. Both he and the nun, who soon afterwards left her community and worked full time on a youth project, showed him deep care and concern, and this became a major factor in his decision to study social work and become involved with urban youth who are at risk. The parish priest, on the other hand, demonstrated 'a complete lack of leadership.'

Tara reported that 'If you feel cared for by somebody, you will take on board what they are saying,' and that the opposite is also true. Based on her experience, there is 'a big connection between care and influence.' Fiona also strongly supports this view. The priest she met at college had a major influence on her life because she felt deeply cared for, listened to, and accepted. It was the first time in her life that she was given the freedom to say who she was as a person and 'to have that affirmed and accepted.' Fiona firmly states that experience is much more powerful than words. When words are 'lived out, you do remember them and they do influence you.' When Brigid was asked if, in her experience, there was a connection between care and influence, she replied, 'Absolutely; you were more inclined to listen to the opinion of those who cared for you, whether or not you took it on board.' This was particularly true in her earlier years, but even now she would definitely be more inclined to listen to someone who cares; 'you know where they are coming from and their opinion counts.' The present influence on Sean's values also came from those who cared most for him.

One of the most unexpected findings that arises out of the in-depth conversations with the five different types of Irish youth is the limited extent to which popular culture influenced their lives during childhood and adolescent years. Apart from Tom, and to some extent Brigid, they were largely sheltered from the cultural invasion that had overtaken Ireland, although on their own admission this was not generally true of their peers. Despite the protection from the winds of change during early and mid-adolescent years, exposure to the lived culture of the city and university quickly challenged inherited beliefs and values and became a dominant influence in their lives.

Progression to tertiary education seems to be accompanied by extensive travel. This begins during the long summer vacations and a whole year of travel often follows immediately after graduation. This is a new feature of Irish youth culture that is having quite a profound influence in forming young people's outlook on life. According to Brigid, the present generation of Irish youth travels very extensively and this has been 'a major influence – in fact, probably *the* major influence' in her life. Among the people and circumstances that have most influenced her beliefs and values are those she has encountered in different parts of the world, from Europe to Australia and from Indonesia to the United States. 'Just meeting people from completely different backgrounds who have been brought up in completely different ways and living in societies that are completely different than traditional Irish society' had a huge impact on her life. Tara's interviews took place in the United States while she was *en route* to Australia in the course of a whole year of travel. When asked to describe life as a young woman in contemporary Irish society, she replied: 'At the moment it is great because I am travelling and having a great time. I have no responsibilities – at the moment it is: have a good time and see the world and enjoy myself.' Tara said that one of the things that gives most meaning to her life at present is being happy as she is, 'not knowing what lies ahead, just going with it and seeing what happens.' This, indeed, reflects a postmodern outlook on life. At the present time, young Irish people are travelling to an extent that was inconceivable in their parents' generation and in doing so they appear to be developing an increasing appreciation of diversity, another mark of the culture of post-modernity.

Primary Values

Considering the demise of institutionalized religious faith among the rising generation, an attempt was made to discover what five young people value most in life. The conversations revealed that the most treasured value is the family of origin, followed by a present partner for those who are in an intimate relationship. Loving and being loved are core values for these young people. Those who have cared for them are the people who are most important; in Fiona's words, 'those who have shared their journey with me and with whom I have shared my journey.' Friendship is especially prized among this group of young people, friends who will 'always be there' for them. A number of them mentioned honesty as a primary value, and as Tom put it, 'good honest-to-God people' with 'no hidden agendas . . . straight, honest, open, sound people.' All of them are very critical of people who are hypocritical or who judge others.

Freedom of thought and behaviour are highly prized among this group of young people, freedom to find the way to where one is going as well as other people's freedom to do likewise. Companions on the journey are very important, provided nobody tries to impose his or her views on anybody else. Each person must be allowed 'their space and their life.' Life itself and good health are thoroughly appreciated, 'every breath and every moment of life', as are experiences of birth or death. Brigid regards being present at a birth or a death as 'incredibly valuable and as real learning experiences.' Fiona even values the experience of pain and hurt. Anybody who ever touched or hurt her is valued because they have made her who she is. Echoes of a post-modern sensibility appear to be present here. Tom Beaudoin points out that contemporary youth have a keen sense of suffering and of being wounded.[7] Another trait of post-modernity that is revealed in the interviews revolves around the desire to belong to a community where individual freedom is respected.

Only one of the young people, Sean, strongly values his membership of the Catholic Church; this is very important to him. Fiona would appreciate this if the Church became more inclusive, especially of women, and more democratic. When asked directly if she placed any value on being affiliated with the Catholic Church, Tara replied: 'I would not really think about it,' whereas that would be a 'huge value' for her parents. An appreciation of nature and a desire for the restoration of ecological balance is an important aspect of the value system of these young people. Brigid, in particular, reacts against the damage to the environment that has been wrought by the culture of modernity. This is not surprising since she values all of life equally – 'animal life, human life, plant life'. It is noteworthy that Sean is the only one of this group of young people who values personal success that will bring material benefit, but his attitude to this is balanced by other human and religious values.

Meaning-Making in the Lives of Contemporary Youth

What gives ultimate meaning to the lives of the majority of those who participated in this study is a belief that they have a message to bring or a contribution to make in their world. In Brigid's case, this message is proclaimed by the way in which she lives – by careful analysis of everything that she does, by treating everything with respect, and by really trying to 'ascertain a rightness in everything' that she does. This is achieved by 'looking at how things feel inside' and by examining how something affects her spiritually and emotionally. Fiona experiences ultimate meaning in the realization that life is a gracious gift from God, and in the communication of this message to others. She is aware that people do not appreciate the 'wonderful story' of God's unconditional love for them, that they are being loved into life, and consequently, 'are missing out on the greatest news.' She says: 'That is my meaning in life . . . that is what gives my life a goal or direction, that somehow I can just be what my God is for me to these people . . . to show them what the gift of life is, just by being there for people.' The major component of meaning-making in Tom's life centres on 'helping someone to reach the best of their ability.' He admits that he is still searching for ultimate meaning and wonders if there is 'any meaning apart from having kids.' He recognizes that a lot of people are driven by money, wealth, and success, and when they achieve that, he asks, 'What is there?' In his search for meaning, Tom appears to share in the woundedness of postmodern youth culture as he states that 'the nineties was a lonely place.' Tara does not share in this predicament. Her motto is: 'Live life to the fullest.' Family, friends, travel, satisfaction with her chosen profession, looking forward to the future, and just being happy all contribute to meaning-making in Tara's life. Religious faith and being able to converse with God, in good times and in bad, also contributes to life's meaning. Like the others, she, too, feels that she has a contribution to make. She plans to eventually attend graduate school, become a nursing tutor, and thereby change current aspects of medical practice with which she disagrees. This, Tara feels, will also give meaning to her life in the future. Sean's attitude to life differs quite substantially from the other four young people who were interviewed. What is most meaningful to him is to become successful in work or in business and to settle down to a happy family life.

Consideration of the meaning-making dimension of the five youth stories again points to the variation among them. Three of them seem to reflect a post-modernity sensibility, whereas Sean and Tara appear to be living out of a modernist perspective; one wonders about Tara, however, especially when she says that not having her life mapped out and 'just going with it and seeing what happens' is a substantial part of what gives meaning to her existence. None of the five young people mentioned affiliation with the faith community of the Church or participation in the Eucharist as factors in giving meaning to their lives. In fact, with the exception of Fiona, they see no connection between the Mass and everyday living, nor do they remember being taught, in religious education at school, about the integral link between celebrating the Eucharist and discipleship of Jesus of Nazareth. This concept is 'totally alien' to Tom and Tara; she would 'never even have thought about it.' In fact, when asked what meaning the Eucharist has for her (when she does go to Mass), Tara replied: 'I don't know; it is just something I do.' Her attitude toward the Mass seems to illustrate the indifference or apathy that, according to recent survey results, is characteristic of those people who have ceased to participate in the Sunday Eucharist.

Conclusion

As one listens carefully to the stories of five very different young Irish people, it becomes clear that contemporary Western culture has a very significant influence on beliefs, values, and Church affiliation among the rising generation. These stories illustrate much of what is written on this topic and clearly reflect the general trends in religious belief and practice that have been revealed through quantitative research, the results of which were reported in the last chapter. Brigid and Sean reflect the positions of those at the two ends of the religious pendulum; on the one hand, the smaller number who have turned their back completely on the Catholic Church and are not even interested in using it for a socio-religious occasion such as a wedding, and, on the other hand, the majority of Irish rural dwellers who continue to be faithful to the Church and adhere to traditional religious practice, especially weekly attendance at Mass. While they are very different in their outlook on life, Tara's and Fiona's positions lie somewhere between the two extremes. Tara appears to embody the attitude of urban Irish youth, the majority of whom no longer participate in the weekly celebration of the Eucharist out of a sense of apathy or indifference, and just want to live life to the fullest. The ritual of the Mass is irrelevant to their daily lives.

For the first time in Irish history, there are now more lay people than seminarians or canonical religious pursuing the study of theology. Fiona is one of this growing number, many of whom desire an active role in ministry as well as some form of leadership in the Church. This development may be connected to the collapse in vocations to the canonical religious life and the critique of the male-dominated leadership in the Catholic Church, which is so evident in the interviews with Fiona, but is most likely a reflection of the impact of the feminist movement that has spread from the United States to Ireland in recent decades.

One representative of socially deprived urban youth was invited to participate in the qualitative aspect of this research. The analysis of the interviews with this young man is richly revealing of the beliefs, values, attitudes, and above all, the perception of Church that is held by this large sector of Irish society, the vast majority of whom have abandoned the practice of the Catholic faith.

The analysis of the in-depth conversations supports the view widely held in the literature on cultural influence that the manner in which young people experience reality is culture bound, and that their ideas, values, and general attitude to life are largely determined by the type of culture to which they are exposed. Beliefs and commitments change as culture changes and as young people move from one type of culture to another. Parents may succeed in protecting their offspring from popular culture during childhood and adolescence, but it is only a matter of time before they become immersed in the wider cultural ocean with its attendant disruption of inherited beliefs and values. Yet, despite the inevitability of this, there is no evidence from the interviews that any significant attempt was made at gospel-rooted discernment and analysis of culture in the various secondary schools that these young people attended.

One of the areas where there was a divergence between the literature on the impact of contemporary culture on young people's faith commitments, and the experience of those who were interviewed, centered on what Gallagher calls 'faith-deafness.' Gallagher, Warren and Kavanaugh believe that contemporary culture is undermining not only Church-related faith but also the requisite openness that is necessary for believing. While most of these young people either rejected, were indifferent to, or criticized institutionalized religion, they were all open to the religious or spiritual dimension of life, and each one believed in God, however this Being was conceived. One possible reason for this is that, according to evidence in the interviews, most young Irish people are more exposed to popular culture in their early and middle adolescent years than these five were, as well as the fact that the latter were heavily influenced by their parents' faith and values. However, it seems more likely that the conversations with the five participants betray a post-modern outlook and search. They are searching for experiential encounters (especially Brigid, Fiona, and Tom) which the religious institution of the Catholic Church is unable to provide. Some of them even want to recover a Jesus who is 'real' and connected to them rather than to the highly suspect institutional Church.

Beaudoin contends that four central themes characterize the spirituality of post-modern young people: (a) organized religion and other institutions are suspect; (b) personal experience is of great importance; (c) the suffering that they experience has a religious dimension; and (d) ambiguity is an essential aspect of faith.[8] The analysis of the interviews certainly revealed a de-emphasis on, and even a rejection of, organized religion. When it comes to making decisions about beliefs, values, and how best to live, personal experience overrides any other factor. Fiona can integrate the hurt that she experiences into her ongoing spiritual search and Tara turned to God in her struggle to cope with the deception that led to the ending of an intimate relationship. She turned to the One who is 'always there for you.' The willingness to live with ambiguity is also evident in some of the interview transcripts. Fiona, in particular, made decisions on the basis of the creative tension between traditional Catholic teaching and her own contemporary experience.

It appears, then, that while the in-depth conversations with five young Irish people betray elements of the culture of modernity, the predominant sensibility that is revealed is that of post-modernity. Even though Sean does not fit this category he clearly referred to postmodern traits among the young people who he knows. The knowledge gained from the interviews also supports Beaudoin's thesis regarding postmodern youth's inner openness to be part of an appropriate faith community, a community of prayer and ritual, which would be characterized by diversity, openness, inclusiveness, and a minimum of hierarchical structure. Perhaps the greatest indication of the postmodern sensibility that seems to be embodied in the young people who were interviewed is revealed in the supreme importance attached to having 'people there for you' and 'being there for other people.' Groome summed up the cry of post-modern youth in the words 'Will you be there for me?'[9] This phrase or similar words were repeatedly used by four of the five participants throughout the in-depth conversations.

On the basis of the extended interviews held with five young Irish women and men, it appears that the biggest challenge facing the Catholic Church in Ireland does not center on the lack of religious faith or lack of openness to the spiritual dimension of human existence. While one should not underestimate the many elements in a consumerist, commodity-driven culture that diminish interiority and block the openness that is a prerequisite for hearing the message of the gospel among large numbers of young people, the greatest threat to meaningful Church affiliation appears to be coming from a postmodern culture that increasingly supplies the framework in which young people live. This is especially characterized by dissatisfaction with religious institutions and their representatives, rampant relativism, pluralism and apathy, as well as a reluctance to take part in ritual that is not deeply experienced.

Notes

1. T. Beaudoin, *Virtual Faith: The Irreverent Spiritual Quest of Generation X* (San Francisco: Jossey-Bass, 1998).
2. M. Foucault, *The Foucault Reader* (New York: Partheon Books, 1984).
3. K. Nichols, *Refracting the Light: Learning the Languages of Faith* (Dublin: Veritas Publications, 1997), p. 66.
4. Beaudoin, op. cit.
5. M. Warren, *Youth, Gospel, Liberation* (Dublin: Veritas Publications, 1998), p. 77.
6. C. T. Whelan and T. Fahy, 'Religious Change in Ireland 1981-1990', in *Faith and Culture in the Irish Context,* ed. E. G. Cassidy (Dublin: Veritas 1996), p. 100.
7. Beaudoin, op. cit.
8. Ibid.
9. T. Groome, Presidential address at APRRE Annual Conference, November 1998.

CHAPTER V

RELIGIOUS EDUCATORS IN DIALOGUE WITH CULTURE

This chapter examines the contribution that significant religious educators have made to the debate regarding the relationship between Christian faith and culture during the twentieth century. It is noteworthy that until recent decades the issue of Christ and culture was tackled mainly by Protestant theologians and religious educators. Indeed, it was not until after the Second Vatican Council that culture became a major theme for the Catholic Church. It is still surprising how few religious educators, until very recently, in either the Protestant or Catholic traditions, have given this topic the attention it deserves. It seems evident that one cannot devise principles for religious education, catechesis or pastoral ministry, not to mention design a programme for these activities, without taking serious account of the cultural context in which religious education and pastoral ministry takes place.

Socio-Cultural Theory

George A. Coe
Coe, writing in 1917, while not using the term 'culture', nevertheless paid careful attention to the social and cultural context that prevailed at the beginning of the twentieth century. This was marked by the effects of the industrial revolution that, according to him, provided a largely unjust social order, industrial conflict, and the clash of nations. He commented on the social inheritance of the American child at this time, which included

> the influence on him of all such things as sights and sounds upon the streets, newspapers, public amusements, political contests, business and social customs; waves of public opinion; home conditions – indeed the influence of every man and every 'man way' that he meets.[1]

Coe believed that society was the primary educator of children and young people as it had a greater influence on them than any other agency.

The main problem that Coe addressed was how to transform Christian education so that it became sufficiently, as well as efficiently, Christian. The theological and christological background to his vision of religious education centred on his belief that the redemptive mission of Christ was concerned with transforming the social order into what he called a 'democracy of God', a term that he substituted for the biblical notion of the 'Kingdom of God'. His theory of religious education was heavily influenced by John Dewey's theory of secular education and he regarded the transformation that the theory of public school education was undergoing at that time as being of the utmost significance for the churches. He particularly welcomed the shift from an individualistic to a communitarian emphasis in the public school system and called on the churches to follow the same path.

Coe believed that the mark of modernity on education had been the emphasis on the child's free self-expression with mental growth proceeding from within outward rather than through accretion. He argued that religious education had been reluctant to assimilate the educational trends of the nineteenth century, mainly because of ecclesiastical authority, which believed that 'The meaning of life was fully and authoritatively revealed in ancient times, so that the central function in religious teaching is to pass on a completed, unchanging deposit of faith.' This was true of Protestantism as well as Catholicism. Considering the momentous and rapid change in the method and content of thought, resulting from the scientific movement during the nineteenth century, the churches were left with a hiatus between an appreciation of free individuality and the content and methods of religious education. Even the 'ideals of culture' were modified as the notion of efficiency and scientific control became more important than the 'cultivated individual' as the measure of success in the educational enterprise.

Coe pointed out that various lines of thought in the milieu of his time converged on the theme of social idealism as a philosophy of life. There was a conviction abroad that social welfare and social progress would give meaning and scope to human experience. Within the public school system, a strong element in the social aim of education was to produce individual self-guidance among students toward the social good of all. It was within this educational and cultural setting that Coe proposed his social theory of religious education. On the basis of Jesus' fusion of divine and human love, he argued for a divine-human democracy as a final social ideal. The aim of Christian education, then, becomes: 'growth of the young toward and into mature and efficient devotion to the democracy of God, and happy self-realization therein'. The mark of successful Christian education would be the increase of effective brotherhood and sisterhood in the world, since the vocation of the Christian was to recreate the social order. Students responded to the call of God by taking on board the social issues of their contemporary culture, and the role of religious education was to enter directly into the social struggles that were present in that culture.

In analysing the industrial society in which he lived, Coe was very critical of its value system, which was characterized by 'regulated grabbing' and 'unrighteous standards.' Furthermore, this situation was destined to continue as each new generation grew up under conditions that constituted a training in selfishness and partisanship. The recipients of religious education were exposed to this social order from infancy upward, thereby soaking up its values, and it was a mistake to postpone in education what could not be postponed in a child's social experience. If one were to master the complexities that resulted from the industrial revolution and press forward a democracy of God, one 'must turn the attention of pupils to many matters that are this side of the biblical horizon'. In doing so, the approach of religious education was not to impose truth, but to promote growth. Coe considered the transference of ready-made thoughts to the mind of another as psychologically fallacious and as an exercise in partisanship. Instead, Coe called for a change from dogmatic and ecclesiastical standpoints in religious education toward a fully social theory and practice, and he claimed that when religious education is embodied in the concept of the democracy of God, 'We have a socially unifying aim to which everything that is truly democratizing and humanizing in state education contributes'.

Furthermore, religious education could influence significantly the humanizing of the state.

Christian education should not be confined to the classroom. Rather, a fundamental aspect of this enterprise is the participation of the young with one another and with their elders in activities that aim at social welfare, social justice and a world society. This is so because the love that is justice demands the whole of a person's social allegiance and a Christian's life work is to rebuild society. In this context, Coe pointed to the 'measureless potential of the family as an agency of Christian education', a belief that is universally held today.

Coe made a clear distinction between society's generally accepted standards and Christian values and said that the social setting of the Sunday school experience should produce in the young person a sense of social contrast between the Church and the world. In terms of Richard Niebuhr's five categories of the relationship between Christianity and culture, Coe may be ranked among the conversionists, that is, those who believe that the Christian task is to transform culture according to the standards of the gospel. In this sense, he belonged to the great central tradition of the Church and, in the words of Niebuhr, believed that 'the Christian must carry on cultural work in obedience to the Lord'.[2] Coe had a positive and hopeful attitude toward society and perceived a unity between the human and the divine. His awareness of the creative activity of God in human life led him to describe God as 'a worker with whom all workers can have fellowship' in the transformation of the social order – the ultimate goal of religious education.

In Coe's theology there was no room for a purely private relationship with God, since human selfhood is conjunct. In religious education, then, fellowship and instruction should be one consistent whole. In other words, young people should experience what they are being taught. Indeed, the comprehensiveness and radicalness of the principle of human fellowship that the churches profess give them a particular function in social education. What is ideally experienced in the life of the Christian community and in its worship should be a model for society at large. Similarly, the religious education curriculum should present demonstrations of the meaning and the power of love. This is doing no more than modelling religious education on the approach of Jesus whose matchless power in telling educative stories 'lies in part in the utter continuity of the life process in his tales with that of his hearers'.

In calling for the transformation of social life toward the highest ideals that could be conceived, Coe said that young people's whole method of ethical thinking must be reconstructed. The most important role of the Church was to instil Christian motives into the growing awareness of children and youth:

> If the Church is to be a perpetual inspiration to the human longing for a humane life, the perpetual organ for the manifestation of the God of love – if this is to constitute the very life of the church, then it must continually stimulate the fresh spirits of the young to make greater and greater demands upon life.

It was Coe's view that the socially integrative power of religion had already positively affected the state, and that the most important task of departments of religious studies was to enable entire denominations to become devoted to, and trained in, the Christian reconstruction of society at large.

In assessing the contribution of George Albert Coe, as a religious educator, to the dialogue between faith and culture, one recognizes his breadth of vision and his far-sighted ideas. He called for an abandonment of 'the doctrine and the principle of the inequality of the sexes'. It would be half a century later before this issue became a central focus of society. It would also be many decades before Coe's vision for religious education became embodied in catechetical texts. The Irish National Catechetical Programme, with its experiential, pupil-centered approach and social flavour, clearly echoes the educational model of Coe. His emphasis on the importance of imagination for social growth among the young is echoed today in the central place that is given to story, art, drama, music, and song in the religious education process. The ecumenical spirit between the churches in recent decades reflects the attitude of Coe, who believed that every religious denomination requires contact with standpoints and practices other than its own if it is to remain healthy. The alternative is religious inbreeding which, in the natural order of things, brings about religious deterioration. 'Love,' he says, 'must keep open house to ideas as well as to persons'. Coe's central emphasis on a just society, on 'a love so divine that it knows no favoured class on the one hand, and no undivine goodness on the other' finds expression, not only in liberation, political, feminist, and black theologies, but also in many religious education programmes.

Coe has been criticized for his inflated social optimism, which was dealt a severe blow in the aftermath of the First World War and later in the pessimism accompanying the economic collapse of 1929. Nevertheless, Coe and other leaders of the Religious Education Association, which was formed in 1903, were highly influential in professionalizing the educational side of religious education in the United States. Coe's position was increasingly challenged during the 1930s and eventually H. Shelton Smith's *Faith and Nurture,* published in 1941, moved the focus away from the fixities of Coe and his colleagues and toward a new search for the most appropriate context for faith formation.[3] While many people had difficulty with the experience-centered approach of Coe, his emphasis on the cultural context of religious education became a key issue in the anthropological approach to this field in the second half of the twentieth century.

Socialization Theories

C. Ellis Nelson

C. Ellis Nelson is among the first religious educators to make explicit reference to the effects of culture on young people and to take serious account of the contemporary concept of culture in the task of religious education. Ellis Nelson concluded from his study of cultural anthropology and sociology that what these social scientists described as the socializing or acculturation process is similar to the way in which faith and its meaning is passed on by a community of believers. His main contention is that 'Religion at its deepest levels is located within a person's sentiments and is the result of the way he was socialized by the adults who cared for him as a child'.[4] While he believes that faith is communicated by a community of believers in much the same way that cultural communication takes place, it is pointed out that this way of communicating Christian faith is complex because the source of direction for Christian faith comes from outside the culture.

Nelson shares the view of all commentators on contemporary culture in recognizing that culture determines the attitudes that are decisive in shaping a person's self-identity and values. He raises the question, then, as to how a Christian, who is a product of the culture in which he or she lives, can develop a way of life that is somewhat different from that culture. While there are no easy answers here, searching questions need to be asked so that religion does not end up being at the mercy of the contemporary cultural value system. Most people tend to avoid examining the unargued assumptions that come from culture because these are highly charged with emotion and because the average person has difficulty in understanding culture. Ralph Linton put it graphically when he noted that for a person to discover culture would be like a fish discovering that it is living in water.[5] Nelson says that if faith in God is to lead to a different life-style, the substance of culture has to be subjected to critical examination. This view is echoed in the perspective of more recent commentators such as Gallagher, Kavanaugh, Warren, and Metz, referred to in Chapter II.

The importance of cultural discernment is highlighted by Nelson's emphasis on the determinative influence of culture on a person's life. From the moment of birth, a child is surrounded by culture. Long before he or she has reached self-consciousness, selfhood is shaped by culture. 'What is unknown is that culture is internalized in persons and institutionalized in society. Culture is the meaning of life that is transmitted to others, especially children.' The world view of a particular culture is mediated directly to children by those who nurture and socialize them, and it becomes an integral part of their self-understanding. 'Imitation is the method by which a person appropriates the style of life of the group in which he comes to selfhood'. The set of behavioural patterns that evolve from the style of life are the means by which specific life situations are met and handled. The values of a child or young person, then, are largely an extension of the values of the nurturing group. Children appropriate the values and world view of parents and other significant adults who nurture them and develop their self-identification in culture.

> The child does not come into self-awareness and then discover culture; he finds and defines himself in a particular culture . . . the appropriation of his parents' way of seeing and living is built deep into his personality – partly unconsciously – and it permeates his whole being.

In this regard, symbols that define and explain life play a very important role.

In pluralistic societies, such as those in the western world, culture and religion vie with each other in claiming to answer the question regarding the meaning of life. Culture, then, is the reality with which one must deal in order to be influential in shaping the values of individuals and society.

Ellis Nelson is of the opinion that, even though the family is a very important agent in the communication of Christian faith, one cannot work out a system of Christian nurture based on the family alone 'because the family is more an agent of culture and society than it is an independent unit'. This is especially so in the case of the middle-class family which is 'so closely allied with, and so responsible for, the secular culture'.

Nelson proposes that since Christianity and culture each offer a world view and a set of values, Christian education could use the same natural process in passing on beliefs and values by moulding individuals, informal groups, and society. Because a similar process of socialization operates with each religious tradition as in society generally, 'Efforts to communicate the Christian faith should be planned to use these natural and powerful processes more deliberately'. He points out that an important function of religious education is to develop young people's awareness of the culture that surrounds them and to help them become more sensitive to the leading of God's Spirit in their everyday lives. Writing from within the Protestant tradition, he proposes that it is necessary to go back to the Biblical revelation in order to transcend the cultural situation in which we live and thereby shed light on the present.

Ellis Nelson emphasizes the communal nature of the Church and regards faith as 'a concomitant of human association'. When people are committed members of the Church, they are able to develop a sense of solidarity in Christ through which faith is nurtured and strengthened for the task of transforming culture. This is particularly important in the case of parents, as the surrounding culture can erode their best desires regarding their children. While they may be effective in shaping moral character, 'unless the church shapes the mind and heart of the parents, the family goals will not be different from those of the surrounding society'. In this regard, faith should be identified with the present experience of people, and Christian education should be closely related to evangelism, which is about personal conversion to Christ. Since the primary purpose of religious education in the Church is to inculcate faith in Christ, 'we must focus our past on the present'. Only insofar as faith is vitally related to what a person is struggling with here and now does it have any real significance. This means that static faith is of little use, and religious education must enable believers to reformulate their faith with a meaning that will make sense of contemporary culture.

In dealing with the Christian Church's ability to interpret its situation in contemporary culture, Nelson spells out his understanding of how an entire faith community can be critically conscious. His most significant contribution to the faith-culture dialogue is his reference to the parallel between the socializing process that cultural anthropologists describe and the way in which faith and its meaning are transmitted by a community of believers. Through a better understanding of the acculturation process in society generally, the Christian community can make a more deliberate use of this natural procedure in passing on its beliefs and values to each new generation. He points out that any meaningful discussion of the communication of Christian faith must bear in mind that culture transmits a world view and a set of values and that these elements are the real forces that shape people's lives. By examining the natural process of cultural transmission it is possible to see why the values of a particular culture are so deeply embedded in people, why they are so completely a part of emotional and intellectual make-up, and 'why the culture we absorb controls our interpretation of life'. An understanding of this basic phenomenon contributes to a better grasp of the problems associated with communicating Christian faith. While it is true that culture is appropriated informally as children and young people absorb the way of life around them, Nelson reminds us that there is also a deliberateness that accompanies informal interaction and that there is clear instructional activity between parents and children. This is not confined to so-called 'primitive' cultures; rather, in relation to one of the key values of contemporary western culture, that of success, there is very deliberate activity on the part of parents, schoolteachers, and other significant adults in order to inculcate this value in young people. Because values are related to changing social conditions, Nelson emphasizes the importance of, not only continuously appraising the values of contemporary culture, but also of being deliberate in communicating the Christian vision of life to children and young people.

Even though Ellis Nelson writes from a narrowly Protestant perspective (he even cites the interdenominational community in Taizé, France, as an example of a primary Protestant religious society, whereas its very *raison d'être* is ecumenical!), he does make a significant contribution to the religious education enterprise in contemporary culture. He is open-minded within his own tradition. His emphasis on practical theology and on the interaction of the Biblical and historical tradition with the living, human situation, applies to all Christian churches if they are to be relevant to the life experience of young people today. In an age when many of the rising generation claim to be Christian while rejecting institutionalized faith, his rejection of a purely private Christianity as a perversion of the New Testament understanding is challenging to those who claim individualistic discipleship of Christ. Finally, Ellis Nelson's emphasis that faith is communicated by a nurturing community of faith and that the meaning of faith is developed by its members in relation to contemporary culture, provides the religious educator with a resource for rethinking the Church's life, as well as its educational and pastoral ministry.

John H. Westerhoff, III

In his initial writing on religious socialisation as a response to contemporary cultural influence, John H. Westerhoff focused descriptively and analytically on the interface between religion and culture.[6] His primary interest is in effective religious education and faith formation and he recommends a new point of departure for religious education, which should be approached by reflecting on the process of cultural transmission or socialization. He says that if the *General Catechetical Directory* of the Catholic Church is taken seriously, 'religious education will begin to focus upon intentional religious socialization'.

Since no definition of religious socialization exists, Westerhoff attempts to define what this concept might mean. 'Religious socialization,' he writes, 'is a process consisting of lifelong formal and informal mechanisms, through which persons sustain and transmit their faith (world view, value system) and life-style'. Because sociologists and anthropologists have provided us with a new consciousness of how human beings acquire their understanding and way of life, we can embark on a new holistic educational process, which Westerhoff names *intentional religious socialization*. While he acknowledges the major influence of the family and the early years of child-rearing on a person's faith, world view, beliefs, values and attitudes, and the almost equal significance of the peer group that often socializes young people into emerging values and a new understanding of life as well as new ways of behaviour, Westerhoff is primarily interested in the socialization that occurs within communities of faith. Unless there is a community of faith that supports and transmits the family's Christian vision, religious socialization faces a very difficult task. He believes that 'an intentional community of faith remains the essential key to religious socialization'. Therefore, the great challenge is to enable local churches to become religious communities that transmit Christian faith.

Westerhoff is not in favor of viewing culture as being in opposition to religious faith. Rather, 'religion and culture are intimately bound together'. Just as culture implies a common understanding and way of life as well as a common set of values, so also religion expresses a particular group's way of life, gives its members meaning, and provides them with understanding. Religious institutions that are perceived as having a sustaining and supportive role for people in a particular culture will be participated in and supported. However, when there is disruption in culture, religious institutions can face a crisis. Ireland would appear to be a good example of this phenomenon.

While Westerhoff does not see a clash between religion and culture, and agrees with Dawson that 'any religious movement which adopts a purely critical and negative attitude to culture is a force of destruction and disintegration',[7] he does believe that 'the marriage of religion and culture is fatal to both partners'. His attitude and approach is that the Church should be a community of cultural change whose task is to 'prophetically judge society's understanding and way of life'. While the Church is always immersed in a particular culture, it has the potential to successfully effect significant cultural change as is evidenced throughout its history. Because of the dominating power of culture and the powerful forces of socialization that abound, there is always the chance that the gospel will be adapted and transformed by culture. The Church, then, is 'called and challenged to be a historical agency, under the lordship of Christ, acting in the world to the end that God's will be done and his kingdom come'.

Westerhoff's view is that Christian catechesis should educate members of the Church to assume the responsibility to continue the mission of Jesus Christ in the world today. If this is to be effective education, it must take place in a community of faith that is facing the issues of contemporary culture by becoming involved in actual human struggles and moral issues. He emphasizes strongly the importance of belonging to a religious community in order to live an authentic Christian life and lauds the *General Catechetical Directory* for the central place it gives to the ritual life of the Church in the task of religious education, an aspect of religious socialization that he acknowledges the Protestant churches have ignored in their recent history. He favours the Catholic Church's emphasis on the Church as a worshipping, learning and witnessing community of faith as a way of understanding and approaching the catechetical enterprise.

Westerhoff acknowledges that given the reality of the pluralistic world of which the Church is a part, it is difficult to maintain the distinctively Christian view of life. Therefore, 'mindful community-building and life may be the only way Christians in the future can sustain and transmit their faith'. In this regard, Kennedy Neville comments that the most effective way for a group to preserve and transmit its heritage is through a transgenerational communal life. She supports Westerhoff's emphasis on the importance of ritual when she states that 'within the rites of passage and other rituals are found an intensely powerful mode for enculturation of the individual and the continuity of his or her cultural loyalties'.[8] Ritual and symbols encode the raw data of human experience, give meaning to people's lives, and in the last analysis cannot be separated from the human condition. 'They form the heart of culture'. Therefore, if one is to effect any lasting and meaningful change within a faith community, ritual and symbolic life must be taken seriously. In emphasizing the inseparability of faith from ritual and symbolic life, Westerhoff argues that those who are concerned with the Church's educational ministry need to explore afresh liturgical life as an essential aspect of religious socialization.

Westerhoff deserves to be complimented for taking account of, in an honest and open way, the catechetical implications of the relationship between Christian faith and culture in the second half of the twentieth century. Both he and Kennedy Neville recognize, along with numerous commentators, that religion is an integral and essential part of any culture. Since every culture has common beliefs and a common way of life, 'culture and religion are intricately bound together'. As John Elias points out, when examining the relationship between religion and culture 'a comparison is not made between two discrete phenomenons but between concepts which greatly overlap'.[9] It is a matter of examining the relationship between one part of culture and other elements of the culture. With this understanding of the religio-cultural nexus, Westerhoff makes a strong case for religious education as intentional religious socialization and suggests ways of using the natural acculturation process to bring about Christian faith and commitment.

Westerhoff places strong emphasis on the role of the Christian community in the transmission of its vision and way of life to the rising generation, an emphasis that is receiving increasing attention at the present time. He believes that religious education has to be 'centered on the life and work of the community of faith', since people are socialized 'by the space and ecology in which they live'. The local Church community offers to all its members, but especially the young, a boundless hidden curriculum that is a powerful, implicit teaching force. Therefore, he calls for the renewal of the life and structures of the faith community, beginning with the adult members. This concentration on the renewal and building of new faith communities does not detract from the primordial role of the family as the first and most important socializing agency. It is clear, however, that, due to the powerful impact of contemporary Western culture on the minds and hearts of the rising generation, the nuclear family will be ineffective in transmitting a Christian vision and way of life without the support of a vibrant faith community. Furthermore, since rite and ritual are at the heart of religious socialization, people need the experience of belonging to a group which celebrates sacramentally the presence and action of God in its midst.

In his second work dealing with the transmission of faith in a contemporary cultural context, Westerhoff does not deal specifically with the issue of faith and culture, but continues in his conviction that 'Faith can only be nurtured within a self-conscious community of faith'.[10] In agreeing with a number of significant voices, who during the 1960s spoke out in favor of a broader understanding of religious education, he questions the paradigm that undergirds the Church's educational ministry, that is, the schooling-instructional model. Children come to faith through nurture in a worshipping, witnessing community of faith, but the schooling-instructional paradigm de-emphasizes the processes of religious socialization in the minds of Church educators and members of the parish community. Moreover, the churches have too easily modeled their educational methodology and approaches on that of secular education. This position clearly differs from that of George Albert Coe.

Westerhoff is now more wary of the cultural threat to religious institutions; this encourages them to bless the status quo and nurture people into it through the very act of religious education. For him, Christian faith means belonging to the community of God's chosen people, a radical community of faith, a prophetic community that lives 'a revolutionary existence over against the status quo'. This is the understanding that should guide the Church's life and mission, so that it does not become just another institution in society. In understanding the Church as a significant community of faith,

Westerhoff continues to believe that no aspect of its corporate life is more significant than its rituals, and that worship has to be central to the Church's existence. 'Rituals telescope our understandings and ways, give meaning to our lives and provide us with purposes and goals for living'. This is why, when culture changes, bringing about a change in people's understandings, meanings, and way of life, they tend to stop participating in the old rituals that once inspired and sustained them. Liturgical catechesis, then, needs to become a central aspect of the Church's educational ministry.

As a result of theological reflection, Westerhoff has become increasingly wary of using the term *intentional socialization*. While he still believes it is a helpful concept, it can give the impression that 'We can and ought to be concerned about determining the life and faith of another'. He now questions that, and instead focuses on what it means to be Christian together. He thereby turns attention away from behavioral objectives for others and emphasizes the character and quality of life that should exist in a community of faith. 'Christian faith,' he says, 'implies the need to focus on the mutuality of our engagements with each other, thereby eliminating all categories such as teacher and student, adult (the one who knows), socializer and socializee'. For these reasons he now prefers the term *enculturation* to name the educational method in a faith community. Because people are historical actors who both shape and are shaped by their environments, socialization literature tells only one half of the story, emphasizing how the environment, experience, and actions of others influence us. Enculturation tells the other half, with its emphasis on the process of interaction between and among people of all ages. Westerhoff believes that it is the nature, character, and quality of these interactive experiences among people within a community of faith that enable it to acquire, sustain, and transmit the Christian vision and that best describes the means of religious education. Enculturation, unlike most catechetical literature, de-emphasizes what one person has to bring to another and focuses on a dialogical relationship between equals.

This demonstrates a certain development, but not a radical change, in Westerhoff's approach to religious education and culture. He is more wary of the possibility of the domestication or acculturation of

Christian faith, with the consequent loss of its prophetic and transformational character. This danger is being adverted to by many commentators at the present time and is a growing threat in contemporary Western culture. Westerhoff continues to question the schooling-instructional paradigm as an adequate means of addressing the catechetical needs of both the small and large Church and he still favours the processes of religious socialization as an alternative. However, his self-questioning regarding the validity of 'intentional religious socialization' lacks clarity, as he is still convinced of the indispensability of a 'self-conscious intentional community of faith' for effective religious education. Perhaps it is better to understand his enculturation vision as an adaptation and an interactive interpretation of the concept of intentional religious socialization. Westerhoff shares the opinion of Ellis Nelson in recognizing that a system of Christian nurture cannot be designed on the basis of the family alone, but that active participation in a counter-cultural self-conscious community of faith is essential for living and transmitting the Christian vision of life. While it does not seem necessary for the Christian community to be countercultural, unless all culture is bad, it is noteworthy in this context that there is a growing awareness today that to be a Christian means to be in community with other disciples of Jesus for the task of furthering the reign of God.

Berard L. Marthaler

Marthaler proposes a socialization model as a comprehensive way of understanding the goals, objectives, and methods of catechesis.[11] Recognizing that the socialization process was operative from the earliest days of the Christian community and was the model underlying Horace Bushnell's idea of Christian nurture, he acknowledges its more overt use by Ellis Nelson and even more especially by Westerhoff.

Before dealing with religious socialization, Marthaler explores the notion of socialization as understood by sociologists, anthropologists, and psychologists. Although the term began to appear in the writings of social scientists during the second half of the 19th century, he agrees with Westerhoff that it was not until the 1930s that it came to be used in its present sense. While numerous definitions of socialization abound today, 'there is a common denominator in all the descriptions and theories, namely, the interaction of an individual with a collective'. Because socialization is interaction, it is important to stress that while every human being is consciously or unconsciously a product of socialization, this process does not involve one-way influence only; rather, a person is both influenced by and influences the group of which he or she is a part.

In endeavoring to understand the development of the individual as a social being, psychology places emphasis on the consciousness of a self in relation to other selves. But despite its major contribution toward a better understanding of human development, it has, according to Marthaler, largely ignored, with the exception of Erikson, the crucial influence of social interaction and the transmission of culture. Sociology, on the other hand, concentrates on group relationships and the manner in which they influence a particular person. It is concerned with the family, school, church, mass media, and other agents of socialization. It understands socialization as 'the process whereby individuals are assimilated into, and brought to conform to, the ways of the social group to which they belong'. Anthropologists have a more basic understanding of socialization than sociologists. For them, culture is the key word and they even use the terms enculturation and acculturation as synonyms for socialization. Understood as a comprehensive symbol system, culture gives meaning and value to all aspects of social living. Therefore, the task of the anthropologist who sets out to study the socialization process is to understand how a culture is transmitted from one generation to another by means of the symbol system. Marthaler points out that even though psychologists, sociologists, and anthropologists use different methods and approaches, they complement one another by focusing on different aspects of the process of socialization.

Marthaler cites Berger and Luckmann to show that socialization takes place through a fundamental dialectic in three 'major moments': externalization, objectification, and internalization. When one appreciates that a human being cannot but put a stamp on the world in which he or she is situated, externalization becomes an anthropological necessity. Even though a human being's relationship to a particular environment is a given, it is not permanently fixed.

Humans strive to put their own shape on the world and to make it fit their own needs. This is how culture develops, and while it becomes 'second nature' to people, it is also separate from them in the sense that it is a product of their own activity and creativity. A particular culture can only be preserved and transmitted to a new generation if a society has the ability to maintain specific social structures and ideals. Seen in this light, culture is not a fixed entity and much depends on people's drive to externalize their needs and desires.

Objectification is a corollary of externalization in the sense that 'socially constructed reality takes on a facticity of its own,' consisting of objects, patterns of behaviour, and meanings that are capable of resisting the desires and designs of their creator. As a carrier of meaning, language is a special case of objectification. It objectifies the shared experiences of a community and makes them available to all members, both in the present and in the future. While meaning is constitutive of the human world today, Marthaler points out that 'Historically, religion, philosophy and art have provided the most important symbol systems in the social construction of reality'.

Internalization occurs when a person reassimilates into his or her consciousness the objectified world of meanings. Although human beings are born with a proclivity toward socialization, this happens only to the extent that they internalize the values and attitudes of the milieu in which they find themselves. Because socialization involves a sharing of common meaning and values it forms the basis through which members of a particular group understand and communicate with one another.

Identity results from the dialectic between an individual and society. A people's self-image and world view are formed by the cultural patterns that they experience and the social institutions that influence them. An individual's social identity reflects the influence of parents, teachers, and at a later stage, one's peer group. Even if an adult ends up with a different self-image from the one he or she was socialized into as a child, childhood experiences leave a lasting imprint. An important way in which society continues the socialization process is 'by encouraging the socializees to appropriate as their own the symbol system that embodies the meanings it shares and gives expression to its values and attitudes'. Symbols that are carriers of traditions and meanings speak to the affective as well as the cognitive dimension of the person. It is the nature of religious symbols in particular to embody and disclose the ultimate meaning of human existence. Because they are so interwoven with one's self-image, an individual who has internalized them has no personal identity without them. Marthaler echoes Erikson's 'eight ages of man' when he says that the socialization process is never completed. The dynamics of externalization, objectification, and internalization continue through the life-span of each human being.

In applying the fundamental dialectic of socialization to the specifically religious sphere, Marthaler notes that a contemporary Christian experiences a world already externalized by previous generations of Christians who shared a common faith. Furthermore, the contemporary Christian 'comes to know it as an objectified world of structured meanings and patterned behaviors that he/she is expected to internalize'. The socialization model of religious education takes everyday human experience as its starting point. Christian catechesis begins with the phenomena at hand. For example, it is interested in how the early Christians came to believe and act as they did, only insofar as this throws light on how men and women today come to believe and behave as they do.

Following the lead of social scientists, students of world religions, and Christian theologians, Marthaler makes a distinction between faith and beliefs. Faith is a basic orientation, a free response to a gracious gift, and specific beliefs mediate its meaning. It follows that socialization into a particular religious tradition is more a matter of belief than of faith. However, catechesis or education in faith can awaken, nourish, and develop the seed of faith. The task of catechesis is to uncover the mysteries hidden beneath the surface of everyday life and to transmit the wisdom and tell the story of a particular tradition. The experiential and anthropological approaches in contemporary catechesis endeavor to build and reinforce the Christian heritage by integrating the faith story with daily human experience.

Marthaler names three objectives of the socialization model of catechesis: growth in personal faith, religious affiliation, and the maintenance and transmission of a religious tradition. These parallel fairly accurately the primary interests of the psychologists, the sociologists, and the anthropologists in their employment of the socialization model.

The Christian community believes that it has a message of immense value, which it is obliged to transmit to successive generations.

> In the language of socialization, the Christian community believes that it has a responsibility to impress its institutionalized meanings and values powerfully and unforgettably on its members.

He points out that while the early Church did not use the language of socialization, it was, in fact, consciously 'socializing' its members, and formal instruction played only one part, albeit an important one, in the socialization process.

In contemporary western culture, which is characterized by rapid change and cultural upheaval, catechesis has the task of holding together a shared vision of reality that gives the Christian community as a whole and each of its members a sense of identity. This means that education in the faith involves sustaining the framework of meaning and value that helps Christian communities and their members to interpret human existence, and pattern their living according to the standards of Jesus Christ and the early Church.

Marthaler echoes the view of Ellis Nelson and Westerhoff in emphasizing the importance of religious affiliation. He reminds us that one of the goals of Catholic religious education is to build community. This points to the insufficiency of either juridical membership of the Church or the vague sense of belonging that characterizes the position of many Christians today. Building community means the socialization of members into an ecclesiasal community, the primary symbol of which is the eucharistic assembly, which emphasizes both unity and Catholicity.

The third objective of the socialization model of faith education is to promote growth in personal faith. Even though faith is nurtured primarily in the context of a community of faith, Marthaler acknowledges that it is, nonetheless, a personal grace that involves a personal encounter with God. Faith has both an intellectual and an affective dimension and it implies knowledge, understanding, loving, valuing, caring, and feeling. Since faith involves one's whole being, catechesis seeks to address the whole person, taking account of 'the person's natural disposition, ability, age, and circumstances of life'. It is in this context that Marthaler refers to the relatively new phenomenon of faith development. He finds Fowler's research helpful in understanding catechesis as a dimension of the socialization process and he believes that Fowler's six-stage schema supports the notion that growth in faith is inextricably connected with socialization.

One of the values of Marthaler's work lies in his keen insight into the fact that unless an institution has a clear grasp of the environment in which it functions, particular strategies and tactics are difficult to evaluate. The Church or any one of its members cannot ignore the cultural context in which agency functions, or the ordinary process of socialization as described by sociologists and anthropologists, and hope to be effective in the work of religious formation.

Marthaler is convinced that the socialization model provides both a way of understanding what much of catechesis is about and also a clear basis for planning catechetical programs. Ultimately, the success or failure of catechetical initiatives will be judged by the effectiveness of the socialization process.

Ellis Nelson, Westerhoff, and Marthaler seek to combine education and faith formation in the context of a nurturing community. They ask, in the words of Warren 'if the life of the community could be centered in the scrutiny of contemporary culture in the light of religious meaning'.[12]

Cultural Analysis and Religious Education

Michael Warren

Michael Warren acknowledges that everything he has written in recent years has been heavily influenced by his study of culture. He regards culture as *the* intellectual issue of the present age, something it will continue to be into the foreseeable future, and a decisive matter for religious communities. He sets out to lay the ground work for a methodology of 'cultural agency.'[13] In other words, he is advocating that all people, especially educators and those involved in the promotion of good human and religious values, talk back to culture by judging, evaluating, and acting vis-a-vis signification. He approaches this task from the perspective of a religious educator.

Warren is preoccupied with what attracts the attention of young people, and in the task of influencing them toward religious understanding and insight has become aware that a religious tradition functions 'as only one among many influences, and in many cases, a weak one'. The key influence comes from the mass media. The rapid development in mass communications has changed not only the means by which reality could be imagined but has made the imagination of life more tangible and dramatically vivid. Those who propose to youth various ways of imagining the possibilities of life wield special influence as their means of communication far excel any other that exists. While acknowledging that a person's vulnerability to certain imaginations of the self may be based in the psyche, Warren states that 'The actual production of various imaginations is less a psychological than a social reality, the end result of networks of persons and agencies seeking to imagine the world of the young'. Understood in this way, influences on the young are neither inevitable nor inexplicable. They are the result of social production and, despite their complexity, are open to careful scrutiny. This means that influences operating through television, radio, films, music and song, advertising, and fashion can be exposed and analyzed.

When one comes to understand the social production of the imagined world for the young, it is possible to see how the Christian community can become a zone of influence among many others. In particular, the Christian Church offers a powerful imagination of life, based on the vision of Jesus the Nazarene, an imagination captured in the symbol of the reign of God. The challenge facing the Church today is to find a way of effectively offering 'a compelling religious imagination of life in the face of other agencies offering attractive alternative imaginations'. Warren is preoccupied with this problem. The viability of a particular imagination will be determined by whether or not people are willing to buy into it and accept the consequences of doing so.

In order to find a systematic, theoretical approach to the various influences shaping consciousness and behaviour in the present age, Warren has examined various theories of culture, but it is clear that he is most influenced by the writings of the Welsh sociologist, Raymond Williams. In building on his understanding of culture, Warren focuses on a specific aspect of culture: the way in which electronic communications shape the human world of meaning. He is convinced that cultural agency needs to scrutinize and evaluate the imagination of human existence, which is communicated through the electronic media, and that critical religious thinking should examine the procedures by which that imagination is created and fed into the human meaning system.

Following Williams' lead, culture is understood by Warren as an active system that produces meaning rather than a static reality involving the vague network of a society's values and meanings. This leads him to focus on the production of signification rather than on its consumption, because unless the system by which meaning is produced can be understood, it cannot be analyzed or evaluated. Furthermore, when people understand how cultural production works, individuals and groups can move beyond being passive consumers of other people's significations. They may even become the producers of meaning themselves, first by questioning what is being audio-visually communicated and then by reimagining life on the basis of a more worthy human or Christian vision. One must understand, however, how culture is produced and how this is related to cultural consumption in order to deal with culture and electronic communications.

Warren uses the term cultural agency as a way of thinking about, and responding to, electronically communicated messages, and he cites Paulo Freire's notion of 'cultural action' as a kindred concept. Freire believed that most people adopt a stance of powerlessness and passivity in the face of a system of meanings and are not aware of the possibility of cultural activity through questioning and maybe even restructuring the system of meanings. Warren's term connotes the continuing possibility of making judgments and then decisions about what one sees and hears via electronic media. 'Cultural agency,' he says, 'is a matter of knowing – or working to know – which aspects of the meaning system one will accept and which aspects one will resist'. Full cultural agency has two aspects; on the one hand, it actively looks at and makes decisions about the meanings and values created for public consumption, and on the other hand, it is actively involved in examining and judging the channels by which these meanings and values are communicated. From this perspective cultural agency embraces cultural analysis: 'the ability to bring cultural products and their latent imagination of life before the tribunal of judgment to assess their value or appropriateness'. Warren agrees with Freire's belief that each person's vocation is to be a subject of his or her own destiny and he is anxious to provide them with a creative way of responding to the cultural oppression that may come from electronic communications.

Turning more specifically to the question of culture and religious traditions, Warren reminds us that most of the stories children hear today are told through the medium of television rather than by their parents. Moreover, each faith tradition has a story to tell the rising generation in order to capture their imagination and direct their vision of life in a compelling way, but this story often clashes with the vivid stories told in the various media. The result is that the electronically imagined world can be in direct conflict with the world that is seen through the lens of religious faith. This seems to be why Pope John Paul II has defined oppression in the First World as mainly cultural, in the sense that it involves a system of values and signification.

Warren shares the opinion of Westerhoff, Ellis Nelson, and others, that religion is a culture that exists within a wider culture. It represents a distinctive zone of signification somewhat paralleling the way that culture is a signifying system. Thus, while a particular religious group must both affirm its specific vision of life as well as all the authentically good values found in the wider culture and be in dialogue with these values, there exists a tension because there are two cultures, each desiring allegiance. Each claims ultimacy for its meanings, but because of the implicit nature of the wider culture's claim, it is more covert and therefore harder to resist. When the wider culture's covert ultimacy is vividly expressed through the medium of electronic communications, religious faith often experiences a crisis. This may not be immediately obvious, since people may take life's ultimate meaning from the wider culture rather than from a religious vision while continuing to 'practice' their faith. One of the dangers facing Christianity in the Western world is that of capitulation to the wider culture, either by pushing religious commitments aside or by reducing religious values to the point where there is no longer a cultural clash. Warren recognizes that the struggle between the church culture and world culture has been a perennial one, but he points out that it is especially difficult in contemporary Western culture to maintain the vision of Jesus, since social status, success, and domination are highly valued and continually reinforced in electronic narratives.

When faced with the culture of fast-moving data and images produced by the electronic media, religious groups, Warren contests, will have to become centres of cultural resistance to whatever is unacceptable to their world view. He believes that resistance is integral to any true form of cultural agency and compares this to Gutierrez's understanding of the type of spirituality of resistance needed by the poor and politically marginal people of Latin America.[14] In this way, religious groups can become zones of signification, their rituals enabling them to focus attention on the vision that directs their lives. In the pursuit of a religious vision (for example, the gospel vision), life structure and the imagery that supports it have particular significance. A religious culture of resistance needs to be grounded in a life structure, or patterned ways of living, that encapsulate an alternative vision of life. Equally, this life structure must be supported by a parallel way of imagining the world. If life structure is to change, images must change in a corresponding way.

Warren makes a very valuable contribution to the dialogue between religious education and contemporary Western culture by focusing specifically on the shifts in the material condition of communications that occurred during the second half of the 20th century. He recognizes that in order to understand any social pattern, one must grasp its material conditions of communications and that the social order that culture communicates is shaped by the signifying system of that culture. One of the advantages of viewing culture as a signifying system is that it connects religion and culture, since religion is also a signifying system. It requires more intentionality and more energy to maintain a religious signifying system in contrast to a cultural one, but as Warren points out, when a group does embrace its religious meanings as ultimate, 'It stands in a place from which to judge its own society and culture'. This should not happen in an antagonistic way, but rather through sharing the message of Jesus in narratives that challenge the ethical assumptions of contemporary culture. Indeed, any sweeping dismissal of mass culture 'dismisses in the same gesture any serious possibility of critique'.

Warren compliments Pope John Paul II for his critique of culture as a system of signification but he calls for this to be complemented by new approaches to cultural production in the Church itself. What is true of the human person as co-producer of the world of meaning in the secular sphere should also be true of the world of religious meaning. Warren is here articulating the views of many members of the Catholic Church who feel excluded from the Church's processes of the production of meaning. While *Christifideles Laici* has many glowing passages about lay participation, there are other passages, overlooking the differences between cultural production and cultural reproduction, that claim that 'True agency remains in the hands of an elite, who by their very nature cannot be contested'. The experience of working with youth supports Warren's view that the most successful youth ministry occurs when young people are provided with the opportunity to become co-producers of the religious culture in which they stand.

It is important to point out that Warren does not see a total clash between religion and culture; rather, only certain features of the religious and secular signifying systems clash with each other. Just as there is need to critique their religious systems, Christians and other religious people should also appreciate the positive humanizing elements in the secular culture. This position echoes many elements of the Vatican II document *Gaudium et Spes*. Warren's main purpose in looking at the dynamic of religious education and culture is to enable people to use their religious vision as a lens through which culture can be viewed and evaluated. He names this as cultural agency, that is,

> The ability, first, to think about how meaning is created, in whose interests it is created and what sort of rendition of reality it is; and the ability, second, to make judgments about the meaning presented to us, using aesthetic, ideological and religious criteria.

Warren offers to religious educators and those involved in youth
ministry a way of transcending the powerlessness that many people
feel when confronted with the powerful electronic means of
communicating a culture that is often alien to religious truth. By
understanding the processes through which the production of
meaning occurs in contemporary western culture, a human face is
given to this culture. This in turn empowers people to embark on
cultural analysis, beginning with careful education. Those who live
within a religious community that embraces a distinctive vision of
reality will have a particular advantage in carrying out this task. All of
this gives hope to the Christian faith community in a country such as
Ireland where, until recent decades, the wider culture had absorbed
many of the values of the religious tradition.

Notes

1. G. A. Coe, *A Social Theory of Religious Education* (New York: Charles Scribner's Sons, 1917).
2. H. R. Niebuhr, *Christ and Culture* (New York: Harper and Row, 1951).
3. H. Shelton Smith, *Faith and Culture* (New York: Scribner, 1941).
4. C. Ellis Nelson, *Where Faith Begins* (Atlanta, GA: John Knox Press, 1971).
5. R. Linton, *The Cultural Background of Personality* (New York: D. Appleton-Century, 1945).
6. J. H. Westerhoff III, Gwen Kennedy Neville, *Generation to Generation* (New York: The Pilgrim Press, 1974).
7. C. Dawson, *Religion and Culture* (New York: Meridian Books, 1958), p. 206.
8. J. H. Westerhoff III, Gwen Kennedy Neville, op. cit.
9. J. L. Elias, *Religion, Society and Culture* (Unpublished Manuscript, 1999), p. 31.
10. J. H. Westerhoff III, *Will Our Children Have Faith?* (New York: The Seabury Press, 1976), p. 62.
11. B. Marthaler, 'Socialisation as a Model for Catechetics' in *Foundations of Religious Education,* ed. P. O'Hare, (New York: Paulist Press, 1978), pp. 64–90.
12. M. Warren, *Youth, Gospel, Liberation* (Dublin: Veritas Publications, 1998), p. 22.
13. M. Warren, *Communications and Cultural Analysis* (Westport, CT: Bergin and Garvey, 1992).
14. G. Guttierrez, *We Drink from Our Own Wells* (New York: Orbis Books, 1983).

CHAPTER VI

A RELIGIOUS EDUCATION AND PASTORAL RESPONSE TO CULTURAL CHANGE

This chapter explores a possible religious educational and pastoral response to the unforeseen challenge facing the Catholic Church in Ireland at the beginning of the third millennium of Christianity. It also outlines principles that should underpin a postmodern educational and pastoral approach to this new reality.

It is important to state at the outset that a number of possible reactions should be avoided. The first temptation is to ignore the present reality of Church affiliation and practice that has resulted from very rapid economic, social, and cultural change. The decline in Church commitment among Irish people, which was quite gradual in the 1970s and 1980s, has been rapidly increasing in the past decade, and this is especially evident among the rising generation. The inclination to ignore the present state of affairs is especially tempting in rural Ireland where the impact of contemporary Western culture has not been as incisive as in urban areas and where there is still a high level of active Church affiliation.

Second, deploring the new multi-media influenced culture in which the Church finds itself serves no purpose either. Because of the perception that large sections of the media are determined to undermine the role of the Catholic Church in Irish society, much energy is directed toward its condemnation. This negative approach needs to be replaced by a mature engagement with the modern media and a genuine Christian discernment of contemporary culture, recognizing the potential for the inculturation of the gospel message in a postmodern milieu.

Third, the attempt to turn the religious clock backward and restore traditional forms of religious practice, while attractive to certain groups in the Church, will only serve to increase the irrelevance of the institution to the lives of young people, and to alienate those who are creative and visionary. This is not to suggest that past pastoral strategies were necessarily bad; rather, as Holland and Henriot point out, 'We are challenged to live up to the creativity of the pastoral strategies in earlier stages, but our response will be different, precisely because our context is different'.[1]

The present crisis regarding young people's disaffiliation from the Catholic Church in Ireland offers a new opportunity for a creative pastoral response that will incorporate new principles of religious education. Rather than bemoaning the fact that organized religion is declining in influence, the Church should seize upon this new situation as a call to radical renewal of its structure on the basis of the message and ministry of Jesus Christ, the spirit and teaching of the Second Vatican Council, and subsequent post-conciliar documents. Much of this teaching has yet to be thoroughly explored and applied at a pastoral and religious education level. Moreover, Church leaders need to hear the cry of the young generation, listen carefully to what is being said, and respond appropriately. Instead of focusing on the dramatic drop in vocations to the ordained priesthood and canonical religious life, the Church should acknowledge the quite dramatic rise in the numbers of young people pursuing courses in theology and pastoral studies. Many of these are hungry to be involved in ministry and feel frustrated at the lack of encouragement and appropriate opportunities for doing so – a point that was clearly made by one of those who took part in the in-depth interviews which were analysed in Chapter IV. Meanwhile, the Church is losing much goodwill and is depriving itself of the services of young women and men who have the potential to change its image and to renew its youth and vigour in the task of inculturating the Christian message.

Religious educators in North America name young people between the ages of twenty and the early thirties as the postmodern generation. The five young people who were interviewed for the qualitative aspect of this study were chosen on the basis of the literature and survey results that are available to represent, in an approximate manner, the different types of contemporary Irish youth. Their ages ranged from twenty-one to twenty-six, and as was pointed out in Chapter IV, all but one of their stories exhibited strong postmodern sensibilities. It seems appropriate, then, that principles for a pastoral and religious education response should have a postmodern character. Furthermore, these principles may also be suitable for faith formation and development among those who are still strongly influenced by the culture of fading modernity.

John Paul II states that the Church, through the Paschal Mystery, has 'received the gift of the ultimate truth about human life.'[2] It is my conviction that the Catholic Church, with its long and rich tradition, has a vision, captured in the metaphor of the reign of God, which has the potential to offer the rising generation a unique religious imagination of life that can still be a major zone of influence among the many other influences in contemporary culture.

Principles of a Post-modern Educational and Pastoral Response
Recognizing that the term 'post-modern' is used in a variety of ways, these principles are based on the understanding of this philosophical and cultural movement, which was explored in Chapter II. In this regard, it is important to point out that modernism and post-modernism are not two distinct human postures but, rather, that the latter developed out of, and as a reaction to, the former. It particularly reacts against the foundationalism, the narrow understanding of language, the atomism, the division between reason and emotion and the general arrogance that characterizes the culture of modernity. Because of the interconnection between the two philosophical and cultural movements, it is not surprising that contemporary Western culture contains elements of a lingering modernity. However, current literature on this phenomenon, which is borne out by the knowledge and understanding gained from the in-depth interviews, indicate that human existence at the beginning of the third millennium is heavily marked by post-modern sensibilities. Consequently, an authentic and effective approach to religious education and pastoral ministry needs to take serious account of this new reality that is both open to the religious dimension of human experience and yet presents problems for institutionalized religious faith.

The One and the Many: Unity in Diversity
An appreciation of diversity is characteristic of contemporary culture and is affirmed by post-modern epistemology as a reflection of the

diversity of contexts and not as an indication of the holding of erroneous viewpoints. The young people who were interviewed prized diversity and tolerance for various points of view and ways of life, and they had little regard for those who judged others for being different. Brigid's story, in particular, exemplified this. She reported that the more diversity a person is exposed to, 'the more you become aware that there is not any one particular set of beliefs that fits who you are.' Moreover, she described the community of faith that she joined for worship as a 'rainbow church.' Others who were interviewed also appreciated a plurality of viewpoints and celebrated differences. Pat valued many elements of Buddhism as well as many of those in the Christian tradition, whereas Fiona called for diversity within the overall unity of the Catholic Church. This new affirmation of diversity presents a challenge to the Church that calls for an appropriate response. In the words of Karl Rahner, 'We must take the risk, not only of a Church with "open doors", but of an "open Church"'.[3]

If religious education and pastoral ministry are to be effective in the contemporary cultural situation, they need to be based on a fundamental principle centring on unity-in-diversity. This principle embraces diversity, allowing all viewpoints to be accorded value, while at the same time preserving the essential parameters of belief, structure and practice within the Catholic tradition. In this way, the Church can critically embrace the postmodernist perspective and its attending culture of post-modernity in the process of inculturating the Christian message. This principle pertains to the four languages of faith – narrative, doctrinal, liturgical, and moral.

One of the features of post-modernity is its challenge to any one grand explanation of human existence, be it Christian, Jewish, Muslim, Hindu, or Buddhist. Instead, it favours many narratives – different religious voices and traditions that exist and flourish to the degree that they listen to, and respect, each other's stories. The principle of *The One and the Many* may find itself ill at ease in the Catholic tradition. Yet, if the Church is to continue in the spirit of cultural engagement, begun at the Second Vatican Council, there appears to be no other alternative to this fundamental principle at the present time.

A new spiritual path appears to be dawning in our time, one that is more integrative and ecumenical than of old. Its ecumenicity is not confined within the Christian tradition but incorporates the other major world religions as well. Many people are crossing over to other religious traditions and returning to their own greatly enriched. This new valuing of the 'other' is supported in the official documents of the Catholic Church. *Ad gentes* states that 'Christians must learn to assimilate the ascetical and contemplative traditions planted by God in ancient cultures prior to the preaching of the Gospel'.[4] This new religious path, as well as being characterized by ecumenical openness and affirmation, is also ecologically sensitive.

The rediscovery of Celtic spirituality, which is clearly reflected in the interviews with contemporary Irish youth in their reference to nature as a source of spirituality, illustrates that the new spiritual path that is dawning today finds expression in different cultures and religious traditions. This, in turn, is presenting a new challenge to classical Christology and ecclesiology. Just as the Christian story is interpreted in a new way, so too the ecclesial community must re-interpret its own nature and reach bravely toward the new and not yet experienced, to the outer limits, to where its narrative, doctrinal, liturgical and moral languages can travel no further. While the person of Christ will always be central to the Christian interpretation of the new ecumenical spiritual journey, a variety of new languages is needed to express and articulate the doctrines of the Catholic faith in order to balance the classical language which is experienced by young people as tired and stale. The variety of fresh languages also illustrates that truth is not simple or uniform but finds expression in multiple ways.

According to the principle of *unity in diversity*, the language of liturgy should be spoken and celebrated in a multivariate manner, as befits the needs of those who participate in this symbolic activity. Since good liturgical experiences contribute significantly to the formation of a person of faith, and since increasing numbers of young people no longer take part in the ritual that is the summit and source of the Christian life, the creation of meaningful liturgical language and diverse liturgical expression for a postmodern generation is an extremely urgent need. Standing at the end of an age when analytical reason eclipsed symbol and mystery and at the threshold of an era that values the mystical and the spiritual, it will be ironic if contemporary youth are not provided in their own tradition with the experience of transcendence and participative community for which they long. This fusion of tradition and contemporary youth experience can only be achieved if the Church encourages diverse liturgical language and expression.

Perhaps the most difficult implication of the unity-in-diversity principle centres on the language of morality. Quantitative surveys have shown that the percentage of people in Ireland who follow the Church's moral teaching has fallen dramatically, particularly in the area of sexual morality. This was clearly illustrated in the interviews. Tara claims to speak for her generation when she says that nobody believes in, or observes, those moral guidelines any more. Reflecting the rampant relativism of post-modernity, she says that, 'There are no absolute rights or wrongs . . . it depends on each person, what is true for them.' On the other hand, these young people put a priority on love and care, and 'being there' for other people, one of whom equated this with what was at the heart of the message and ministry of Jesus the Nazarene. Brigid, who is most alienated from the Catholic Church, lives out of a morality of care and respect for all of life that is deeply Christian at its core.

The application of the principle of unity-in-diversity to the moral life of young people requires an attitude of openness, listening, and respect (not to be confused with compromise) on the part of religious educators and pastors. Above all, the temptation to return to the inordinate emphasis on sin should be avoided. Fiona's childhood and adolescent years, which were lived on a moral landscape dominated by sin, compounded her experience of failure and adversely affected her human and spiritual development.

Just as story, as a language of faith, is part of a larger narrative genre that is universal in human culture, and doctrine and liturgy belong to the sphere of philosophy and symbol, respectively, so also Christian morality is part of a larger world. The study of human moral life, and not particular Church teachings, should be the starting point in the moral education of young people. One may argue that there is nothing radically new in this, that good Christian moral education always moved from the natural law to the specifically Christian moral code.

But the principle being explored here carries a different approach. Because postmodern youth reject foundationalism and disembodied language, the study of human moral living must begin with the life experience of those to whom it is directed. The careful exploration of human experience can lead to the weaving of a moral web, at once contextualized and embodied, in which the dignity of the human person and ecological sensitivity are paramount. It is a short step from here to recognize how Christian faith reinforces this position through the belief that each human being is an icon of God and that the world is God's creation. Young people may even be enabled to see that their conclusions largely correspond with the Catechism of the Catholic Church, which introduces its moral section by way of the truth that the human person is created in the image of the Creator. However, it is important to remember that formulations become disembodied unless they continually draw life from human experience; there needs to be constant interaction between the two.

From the perspective of young people, the Catholic Church is extremely legalistic; law is the main horizon of moral life. During the interviews the word 'love' was used innumerable times. The experiences of love and care are among the most important in the lives of these young people and yet they do not associate this with Christian moral teaching. One of the challenges facing religious educators and Church leaders is to lead young people to the realization that love is the very being, the very nature of God, that this love is incarnated in Christ and that love is at the heart of Christian morality. A Christian morality that is centred on love is essential to the principle of unity in diversity. Law promotes sameness, whereas love, by allowing true self-growth, promotes variety and leads to unity rather than uniformity.

The principle of unity-in-diversity has a particular place where Catholic moral absolutes are most ignored, that is, the area of sexual morality. This is the sphere where greatest moral change has occurred in just one generation. The parents of today's youth were reared on a morality where sexuality was understood in a narrow puritanical way and the body was considered as the home of evil desires and passions. The body was often presented as the source of evil, lust, and seduction. Many young people wonder at how, in a religion based on the Incarnation, the body could be regarded in such a negative fashion.

This negative attitude toward the body contrasts sharply with the reverence that is shown to sexuality and to the human body by contemporary youth. It is a complete reversal of Catholic moral teaching. If the Church is to have any credibility in this moral area it must strive to redress its former negative attitude consequent upon a dualism that resulted from a false interpretation of Greek philosophy. While a theology of sensual love never flourished in the Christian tradition, there is hope today that the sacred presence of the body will be appreciated in a new way. The revival of Celtic spirituality is a major influence in this development. Young people need to be introduced to this new orientation in the Catholic tradition if there is to be any hope that they will be open to even listening to the Church's voice in the area of sexual morality.

To date, little effort has been made in religious education or pastoral ministry to develop in young people the skill of forming their own consciences. Instead, they have been taught to obey the moral laws of the Church. Since the present generation of youth largely resents absolutes, the only hope of engaging them in a consideration of Catholic sexual morality is to educate them concerning the place that law and conscience play in the moral life, and to give them the skills necessary for freely chosen moral decisions. Fiona's attitude in this area provides a model of what one might hope to achieve under the principle of unity-in-diversity. She states that she would not necessarily go along with what Church authority says, 'just because they are saying it, just because it is a law that is laid down.' Rather, Fiona informs herself about Catholic morality on an issue and comes to a decision on the basis of the interaction between her experience and the tradition, because she says, 'It is only when you look at the whole picture that you really get the best answer and the least selfish answer.' According to this model of Christian moral education, the decisions reached by young people may not always correspond with Church teaching. Nevertheless, it is surely better to engage the rising generation in dialogue with the moral stance of their faith tradition than have them ignore it entirely in the pursuit of truth and goodness.

When considering the principle of unity-in-diversity, it is important to remember that the ultimate push that caused Brigid to abandon the Catholic Church was a priest's refusal to allow for any diversity. Unless the Church is willing to accept the principle of unity in diversity rather than uniformity, there appears to be little chance that it can provide a faith home for a postmodern youth generation. Rahner's assessment is correct when he states that 'a pluralism . . . the constituents of which do not enjoy equal rights dogmatically speaking but do in fact exist in an open Church, need not threaten the real foundations of a dogmatically firm and self-assured Church'.[5]

Engaging Contemporary Culture

Many commentators on the issue of Christian faith and culture point to the importance of enabling young people to engage in cultural discernment, critique, and analysis. According to conversations with young people who attended school in five different regions of Ireland, there was little attempt made to provide them with some skills whereby they could stand back from, and critically examine, the culture in which they already were, or soon would be, immersed. There was certainly no apparent gospel-rooted discernment of culture in religious education classes. If religious education is to be authentic, effective, and relevant to the lives of today's adolescents, one of the principles that should direct its course is that of cultural engagement. The real significance of religious faith is determined by the extent to which it is vitally related to a person's everyday human experience. In this regard, it is vital that religious educators, youth ministers, and pastors avoid the temptation of a sweeping dismissal or condemnation of mass-produced culture, since this prevents the possibility of a mature critique of the implicit and covert forces that determine many values among the rising generation. Instead, a gospel-rooted vision of life should act as a lens through which contemporary culture can be viewed and evaluated.

In his unique contribution to the discipline of education, Paulo Freire has demonstrated that there is no neutral education.[6] It either domesticates or frees people. Although it is traditionally understood as a conditioning process, education can equally be conceived as an instrument for de-conditioning. At present, the Irish education system supports the broader culture in which it operates. A key value in this culture is that of success, and education is driven by the 'point' system, that is, the attainment of the highest number of points in the Leaving

Certificate in order to enter the university courses that lead to the most lucrative professions. As Tom pointed out in his interviews, this leaves little room for any other focus. The current educational approach, then, conditions adolescents to uncritically buy into the broader culture of contemporary Ireland in which Christian values are diminishing in importance.

At the heart of Paulo Freire's thought, there is an experience and a vivid perception that education can be a de-conditioning process. While human beings are essentially conditioned, they are also capable of knowing what conditions them, capable of reflecting on their action and behaviour, and of perceiving their perceptions. Drawing on this insight, the principle of cultural engagement, if applied at secondary and tertiary educational levels, will empower young people to examine the processes that form individuals and society, and to analyse cultural production and the formative influence of culture on people's lives. An enlightened approach to education in contemporary Ireland must surely include this type of cultural engagement in order to counter the uncritical absorption of pre-processed reality by the rising generation.

Considering the widespread concern about the loss of good human and religious values in the European community as a whole, cultural engagement is a worthy objective of the educational enterprise in Ireland. But there is another dimension of the principle of cultural engagement that is vitally important for the Christian churches and other religious institutions, that is, the evaluation of contemporary Western culture from the perspective of the religious imagination of life. The majority of adolescents in the Republic of Ireland attend Catholic secondary schools, and those who are educated in State schools are exposed to a number of religion classes, each of which is generally conducted by qualified religious educators. This gives the opportunity for a religiously inspired discernment of culture as a dimension of the overall principle of cultural engagement. Since this appears to be almost completely lacking at the moment, a formidable task lies ahead.

Recognizing that a religious tradition, such as the Catholic Church, is only one of the many influences, and in some cases a very weak one, on the beliefs and values of contemporary Irish youth, it is not sufficient to focus only on improving the content and methodology of religious education programs. It is imperative that Church leaders and religious educators have a clear grasp of the cultural context in which the religious education and pastoral enterprise take place, if they are to be effective in their ministry. Having come to a good understanding of this environment, the next step is to incorporate a gospel-rooted discernment of culture as one of the main objectives in the religious education curriculum.

The insights of Warren and others point to the fact that cultural influences on the young are neither inevitable nor inexplicable and that they are open to careful examination. In order to be effective in the ministry of cultural engagement, it is important to understand the system by which meanings and values are produced. This requires at least some familiarity with the way in which rapidly advancing technological communications influence the human world of meaning. Having come to a clearer grasp of both the nature of contemporary culture and how many of its meanings and values are produced and communicated, religious educators are in a position to move toward a critique of the surrounding culture, based on the Christian imagination of life. In this way, the religious education class or parish youth group can become a center of cultural discernment and challenge to whatever clashes with its Christian vision of life.

Education, and in particular religious education, which takes account of the principle of cultural engagement, especially as it relates to the fast-moving world of electronic communications, can enable young people to put a human face on that culture and deepen their awareness of what most influences their ideas, values, and general outlook on life. In order to gain the attention of the rising generation, the process of cultural engagement needs to be open-ended and tolerant. The postmodern generation celebrates diversity and reacts against blanket criticism of the world that they inhabit. Therefore, the religious educator or youth minister has to perceive and appreciate the authentically good values that are present in the culture of post-modernity and allow the Christian imagination of life to be in dialogue with these values. While one acknowledges the valuable contribution that has been made by Warren in the area of education and cultural analysis, the principle of cultural engagement being recommended here extends Warren's approach to take account of postmodern sensibilities. During the interviews with Irish youth, Tara showed particular sensitivity toward any criticism of her generation's lived culture, even if it is radically different from the Catholic culture of her parents' youth. The principle of cultural engagement must always begin by an examination and appreciation of what is good and true in the culture of post-modernity, whether that be ecological awareness, openness to the mystical and spiritual, or desire for intimate, interactive community. When young people perceive that many of their values are considered by religious educators and pastoral workers to be implicitly or explicitly Christian, they will then be open to see that other aspects of their culture do not correspond with the Christian vision of life.

Sensitivity to the Feminist Perspective

The feminist movement of the last few decades has had a firm impact on the Irish cultural landscape. This is evident in the fields of politics, economics, education, mass media, and the arts. It is symbolized in the office of President, a role that has been fulfilled by a woman during the last two terms. Perhaps the greatest change that has occurred with regard to women and the arts is the advent of Irish women poets. In the poetic Irish tradition up to recent times, women played the role of motifs for male poets. The advent of Irish women poets has not just added a new poetic voice but has changed the tradition itself. What is significant about this is that women's experience in finding poetic expression goes beyond poetry and the arts and is symbolic of the new role of women in Irish society, one of the greatest single cultural changes in recent decades.

Now that the majority of people who are pursuing the formal study of theology are no longer candidates for the ordained priesthood or canonical religious life, and most of these are women, one is beginning to hear a new voice among the rising generation. This is evident in the interviews, where a young theology graduate is crying out for her voice to be heard in the Catholic Church. Increasing numbers of young women are searching for a voice and a meaningful role in their faith community. It will be a huge loss for the Church as a whole if their voices are not heard and taken seriously. Enda McDonagh writes that

The great absence from the official leadership of the Church for almost two millennia has been that of women. That alone would be sufficient justification for turning to their experience and insight in seeking to understand the present serious crisis.[7]

Two of the women, in particular, who were interviewed pay close attention to the inner rhythm of their days and lives and have a highly developed spirituality that is indicative of the new spiritual path that is coming to birth in the age of post-modernity. It behoves a Church in crisis, both in Ireland and in the Western world generally, to be sensitive to the articulation of a fresh, but deeply Christian and incarnational, spirituality that is dawning at the beginning of a new millennium.

Patriarchal societies tend to be characterized by a kind of dictatorial, cultlike, self-serving domination over others, especially women. Within the Judeo-Christian tradition, the social, political, cultural, and religious fabric of life has been largely determined by men. Today, women's voices are no longer silent. Feminist theology and spirituality are making a very significant contribution to the new human and spiritual awareness that is dawning among a postmodern generation. The new religious path, as well as being characterized by diversity, ecumenical openness and affirmation, is also ecologically sensitive. With many spiritual feminists, ecofeminists and ecologists, Carol P. Christ shares the conviction that the crisis that threatens the destruction of the earth is 'not only social, political, economic and technological, but is at root spiritual' and that 'we fail to recognize our profound connection with all beings in the web of life.'[8] This point is clearly illustrated by the women who participated in the interviews. If one accepts Berry's claim that during the period of modernity, 'dark and limited aspects of Christianity' caused Western society to 'act so harshly towards the natural world,'[9] the Church's contribution to the ecological debate can only be enriched by increasing sensitivity to the feminist perspective. By listening to the voices of young women, such as those who were interviewed, the Church can develop a more creation-centred theology and spirituality that will balance the current redemption-centred emphasis.

Many male theologians have heard the voices of women and are sensitive to the feminist perspective. Sachs writes that 'an authentic Christian anthropology must emphasize the dignity, freedom, equality and mutuality of men and women'.[10] The Magisterium of the Church has also responded. Pope John Paul II in his encyclical *Familiaris Consortio*, noted the offenses against women's dignity that persist in our culture through 'many forms of degrading discrimination'.[11] In other writings he has apologized for the Church's role in maintaining some of these forms of discrimination. In these writings he pleads that 'vigorous and incisive pastoral action be taken by all to overcome them definitively so that the image of God that shines in all human beings without exception may be fully respected'.[12] Words must now be matched by action. An indispensable principle underpinning a contemporary religious education and pastoral ministry is that of sensitivity to the feminist perspective in society and in church.

A new objective of religious education at secondary level should centre on an exploration of the feminist perspective on life generally and in particular should examine women's role in the Church. In the application of this objective in the classroom, on retreats and among youth groups, adolescents can be educated to understand and appreciate what is feminine and what is masculine, what is manly and what is womanly, what is culturally learned and what is biologically determined male-female behaviour. They can be led to value male-female differences and the complementarity of the genders in the Church's role and mission in the world today. Everyone can be encouraged to discover a personally fulfilling way to exercise his or her talents in the pursuit of a common vision while belonging to a community of faith that values equality and diversity.

Seminarians and other young men and women who pursue courses in theological studies are exposed to an almost exclusively classical theology. There is an urgent need for this emphasis to be complemented by a comprehensive treatment of feminist theology. This will encourage healthy dialogue between male and female theological and spiritual perspectives. Above all, feminine perspectives must be respected, listened to, and learned from if the Catholic Church is not to lose the goodwill, support and active membership of the young female postmodern generation, who are becoming increasingly alienated from the Church.

Sensitivity to the feminist perspective needs further application in the pastoral training of candidates for the ordained priesthood. Ideally, this should occur in a mixed gender setting with formal input coming from women as well as men. The majority of religious educators at primary and secondary levels in Ireland are now women and they also have the greatest influence on the religious formation of the young at home. Women, including those in the canonical religious life, exercise a wide variety of formal and informal ministries within the faith community of the Church. Young men who are preparing for official leadership roles in the Church have much to gain from the experience and expertise of these women. They need to listen to their voices and to the voices of their female peers so that pastoral policy and approaches may be enriched and made more relevant in a rapidly changing culture.

Socially Oriented Religious Education and Pastoral Strategy

The alienation of the socially deprived from the Catholic Church in urban Ireland is starkly presented in the results of the MRBI survey that was carried out in January 1998. Since these showed that only 7% of the total population of a socially deprived urban region attended weekly Mass, one may assume that few, if any, of the young generation did so. This alienation of the young urban, unemployed, and low wage earners is clearly illustrated in the interviews with Tom, and is one of the great challenges facing the Catholic Church in Ireland at the present time. Above all, this is a challenge to the credibility of the Church's embodiment of the message and ministry of Jesus the Nazarene and to its new self-understanding of its mission in the world.

Ongoing research in the scriptural field makes it clear that, while the message of Jesus was not a political one, it had definite political implications, especially in regard to the marginalised in society. The heart of Jesus' message is encapsulated in the metaphor of the kingdom or reign of God. The reign of God becomes effective when God's justice is established 'in the special sense of help and protection for the helpless, the weak and the poor'.[13] Jesus was the bearer of a new possibility of human, social and political relationships.[14] Furthermore, scripture scholars agree that there is clear evidence in the writings of the young Church that the early Christian community faithfully interpreted and embodied the message and ministry of Jesus Christ. It recognised that its task was to carry on the misson and ministry of Jesus for the reign of God. The young Church had a keen sense of justice and of the importance of special care for the socially deprived.

As the centuries passed, Christian faith became increasingly privatised, the emphasis being placed on the development of individual faith, the elimination of personal sin and the salvation of the individual soul. As Christian ministry became more and more clercalized, its focus moved from service of the community to service of the Divine Power as an individual. Philosophically, over the centuries (with some exceptions such as Augustine), there was a move towards an emphasis on the contemplative life at the expense of the political life. This led to a very rational and theoretical emphasis in Christian theology.

As a reaction to the heavy focus on the theoretical and conceptual, a major shift has occurred in Catholic theology during the second half of the last century. This has been especially characterized by the emergence of European political theology and Latin American Liberation theology. This new way of doing theology focuses on the practical living out of the Christian faith and is 'directed toward the creation of a better world in the name of the kingdom of God announced by Jesus'.[15] This praxis understanding of Christian faith embodied in political and liberation theology is reminiscent of the practical theologizing that was a mark of the early Church. Classical theology tended to view the social situation as a reality that was determined, whereas Liberation or process theology calls for the reshaping of the world and the re-ordering of the human and social situation of the marginalized according to the demands of the gospel and the prophetic tradition of the Old Testament.

During the last century, there has been very significant development in the social teaching of the Magisterium of the Catholic Church, beginning with the first great social encyclical, *Rerum Novarum*, issued by Pope Leo XIII in 1891. This was 'the beginning of a process that eventually led Church leaders, including Pope John Paul II, to approve of a notion of an option for the poor.'[16] Within the official teaching of the Catholic Church a clear consensus has now emerged regarding the integrity between the proclamation of the gospel and witness to justice.[17] One can decipher significant shifts in the Church's formal teaching, which have followed upon the development of praxis oriented political and liberation theologies.

The Catholic Church's formal recognition of the social implication of the gospel message and of the importance of social praxis gives rise to a new perception of its mission in the world today, especially among the marginalized members of society. However, it is precisely in this context that it appears to be in a paradoxical situation. Its own self-understanding does not correspond with socially deprived urban youth's perception of the Church's role and mission. In Tom's words, 'It does not walk the talk.' While a small number of individual Church leaders have a high profile in poor urban areas, the Church as a whole is not regarded as having opted for the poor.

John Elias says that 'The first step in bringing about personal and social change . . . is to raise people's consciousness about themselves and about the world in which they live'.[18] Education is vitally important in this regard. Tom reported that his social consciousness was raised by a youth leader who had no connection with the Church. It is probable that his experience is repeated in other comparable situations throughout Ireland, as many of the youth leaders who are employed on government-sponsored schemes have little, if any, Church affiliation. Since the vast majority of socially deprived urban youth are now alienated from the heart of the Church's life, there is an urgent need to take community-based practical steps to make its social teaching credible.

A major challenge facing the Catholic Church in contemporary Ireland, where the gap between the rich and the poor is widening, is to find a way of educating the young generation as a whole, and more particularly, those who are socially deprived, in the rich and radical social teaching of the Magisterium as well as in the social theology that has been recently developed. This should not only form a central part of the school curriculum in religious education, thereby educating all adolescents in contemporary Catholic social teaching, but should also be central to any parish-based youth programs. A special effort needs to be made to involve youth groups in the socially deprived urban regions of the country in reflection on their socio-economic experience in light of the Judeo-Christian scriptures, the social teaching of the Church and current developments in social theology. There would seem to be no reason why the praxis-oriented social theology outlined by Dermot Lane could not be applied in concrete pastoral situations in Ireland, especially among those who are economically, socially, and politically marginalized.[19] The perception among the five young people who were interviewed was that little or no attempt is currently made to educate the rising generation in the social dimension of the Christian message. Hence, an important principle of any credible religious education and pastoral strategy is to foster critical social consciousness among the young, based on the message and ministry of Jesus Christ and the social teaching of the Catholic Church.

Following the exodus of the majority of economically and socially deprived urban youth from active membership of the faith community, there is an increasing danger of what commentators describe as the acculturation or domestication of the Christian faith and the development of a bourgeois style religion. In whatever way one names this phenomenon, it is reflected in people who have formal membership of the Christian Church, yet live according to many of the non-Christian values of the prevailing culture. The application of the principle of a socially oriented religious education and pastoral approach can counteract this growing tendency. Christian youth education should challenge all who profess belief in Jesus of Nazareth and belong to his community of disciples to become more aware of the social implications of their Christian faith, to become more actively involved in both domestic and international loving service, especially in the cause of justice, and to become more aware of the ways in which their faith can become acculturated.

Openness to the Stories and Perspectives of Youth

One of the principles that should guide a postmodern approach to religious education and ministry to young people is that of openness to their particular perspectives on human and religious living. I was pleasantly surprised at the willingness, indeed the enthusiasm, of five young people to give many hours of their time (indeed, a number of days) to the interview process in order to share their faith stories. The person who is no longer affiliated with the Catholic Church was as enthusiastic and cooperative as the one who is a faithful member. Each of them had a desire, and appreciated the opportunity, to voice their thoughts and feelings about church membership and religious practice, spirituality, and the influence of contemporary culture on their beliefs and value systems. The interview process revealed that young people today are willing to engage in dialogue with official members of the Church in matters of mutual interest. They want their views and feelings about the Church and religious practice to be listened to and treated in a non-judgemental and respectful manner. Some of them expressed an explicit desire for the Church to listen to their voices. Even Sean, who had a very non-critical stance toward the Catholic Church, would appreciate dialogue with it on some of its teachings and on its engagement with a rapidly changing culture.

The principle of openness to the stories and perspectives of the rising generation applies to many aspects of religious education and youth ministry. In the area of school-based formal religious education, it is imperative that from the beginning of secondary school, adolescents are consulted before any catechetical programme is developed. The present system of piloting an already prepared draft text needs to be replaced by an initial process of consultation with each year group in selected schools that are representative of the entire adolescent population. Only after careful engagement with this age group's experience should a first draft of a religious education programme be prepared. This may then be piloted in a manner that involves careful listening and allows for the incorporation of adolescents' experience in the final text. This process of consultation should significantly increase the chance that religious education programs will be relevant to, and engage, the interest and imagination of secondary school students.

The implementation of the principle of openness to youth perspectives is even more important in universities and other third-level institutes of education. It has been noted in the analysis of the interviews that the chaplaincy or campus ministry department did not impact on those who proceeded to tertiary education after secondary school. These are precisely the Church personnel who have an important role to play in the ministry of listening to youth. As they progress through tertiary education, students develop strong views about many matters and value the opportunity of speaking their minds. The chaplaincy department can respond to this youthful enthusiasm by creating listening forums where students can express their views about any aspect of Church, faith, or spirituality. If these young people feel that their views are listened to and taken seriously, they will be much more likely to become involved in Church-related activities on campus.

The listening principle also has an important place at parish and diocesan level. There is an urgent need for each parish in Ireland to set up a youth forum where the views and experiences of contemporary youth can be aired. This may be facilitated by a youth minister or other suitably trained adult and should include the presence of the parish priest. In this way, the rising generation will feel part of the faith community, influence its vision, and contribute to more dynamic and appropriate liturgies. The parish listening youth forum needs to be accompanied by a similar body at diocesan level. This would be composed of young people representing each parish in the diocese. The idea is that a representative from each parish would bring the views and experiences of local groups to a diocesan forum attended by the bishop. This ensures that a chain of communication exists whereby the voices of the rising generation are heard not only by local Church leaders but also by leaders at diocesan and, ultimately, national levels.

The principle of openness to the stories and perspectives of young people develops Warren's notion of cultural production within the Church. Just as the human person significantly influences the world of meaning in the secular sphere, so also he or she should be allowed to participate in producing the world of religious meaning. Young people, in particular, feel excluded from the Catholic Church's processes of the production of meaning. By listening to, and taking on board, the views of youth, Church leaders can genuinely involve the rising generation in the formation of the religious culture at parish and diocesan level. This will give them a sense of ownership of the Church, something that is sorely lacking at present. One of the characteristics of postmodern youth is that they desire to belong to a faith community that is open to diversity and that they can influence to a significant degree. Without openness to the perspective of the postmodern generation there is no hope that the decline in Church commitment will be stalled or reversed.

Educating in a Mutually Critical Fashion

It had been widely assumed that the 'scandals' involving child abuse by clergy, which rocked the Catholic Church in Ireland during the last decade, were largely responsible for the growing disaffection among increasing numbers of people. As Hanley pointed out, this speculation is not supported by the results of the most recent surveys. While the majority of those who were surveyed believed that the authority of the Catholic Church had been damaged, they appear to distinguish between the misbehaviour of a small number of clergy and the ministry of the majority. There is a tendency to criticize the institution of the Church without letting this affect personal faith.

The criticism of the institutional Church was much more pronounced among the five young people who were interviewed. Yet each of these had very high praise for particular priests. The rising generation clearly distinguishes between the institution and individual leaders who minister in that institution. Furthermore, the Church was not the only institution that was criticized. Tara, in particular, was very critical of the manner in which the media handled the instances of child sex abuse by priests. She felt that it was very biased and unfair and that it used these 'scandals' as an opportunity 'to bring down the Catholic Church in Ireland.' Postmodern youth's penchant for criticism of institutions is not confined to the Catholic Church. The in-depth conversations showed that they are even open to critique contemporary culture, although they are very sensitive to criticism of their own value system.

The principle of educating in a mutually critical fashion is an important one today if the Church is going to be successful in engaging the minds and hearts of contemporary youth. If a religious educator or youth minister focuses attention solely on a critique of secular culture, young people will perceive the Church in a negative light. In order to be credible, Church leaders need to be open to a critique of the religious culture in which they minister, as well as the secular culture in which young people are immersed. The secular culture is not all bad and the religious culture is not all good. Rather than seeing a total clash between religion and culture, religious educators and youth ministers can lead young people to understand that many features of the religious and secular signifying systems complement one another.

Many positive humanizing elements of the culture of post-modernity were revealed in the interviews with the five young people. In particular, they put a high value on love and care, and 'being there for other people.' Some of them claimed that this is what gives most meaning to their lives. These values are at the heart of Christianity and it is incumbent on religious educators, youth ministers, and Church leaders generally to acknowledge these features of contemporary culture and to affirm them when engaging in a faith-culture dialogue with the young. If the rising generation comes to see that the adult Church is not condemning or denouncing the cultural ocean in which they swim, they will be more open to critique many aspects of that culture that diminish good human and religious values.

During the interview process, Tara was very positive about the culture in which she is now immersed, whereas the other four participants were critical of some of its features. Tom said that

> In Ireland we are very much driven by how much we can buy and how good we can look . . . there is a big 'once we are okay, that is an okay attitude.' It is summed up in the saying: 'I'm all right Jack; to hell with the rest of you.' That has come to the fore *en masse* in Ireland.

He goes on to say that contemporary Irish culture is heavily influenced by satellite television, computers, play-stations, and the Internet. 'I think that is where we are going wrong . . . people have become less and less important . . . the machine and the computer have taken over.' He echoes Beaudoin when he states: 'It is kind of artificial reality, the whole thing.' Tom continues to live this reality, but Brigid has stepped back somewhat from it. She acknowledges that 'Everybody is influenced by the surrounding culture to a certain extent, either positively or negatively; it influences their ideas and values.' But while popular culture 'has a big influence on some people, a small number of young people are turned off by it.' She and a lot of her friends 'would be happy to take a step back in time.' They 'react against modern culture and want to go back to a more basic set of values.' Fiona reported that 'Modern culture is great in offering me comforts when I need them, instead of searching for them somewhere else.' But like Brigid, she can 'stand back and see its falseness.' Even though life has changed and Sean is 'living at a faster pace,' he still likes to go back to his family and friends. He stated: 'I always like to go back to it; I will not say to the old time, but you think as much of that as you do the current stage of our life – money, cars, and what not.'

It appears from the conversations with those who were interviewed that young people are open to critique the culture in which they are immersed. It is also probable that within any gathering of the young, whether formal or informal, there will be some people who are ready for contemporary cultural critique while there will be others, like Tara, who do not immediately notice any flaws in their experience of living today. A religious educator, youth minister, or pastoral worker can facilitate constructive dialogue in educational settings that will empower the rising generation to evaluate their cultural experience in the light of the Christian vision of life.

Since post-modern youth are critical of institutionalized religious faith, religious educators and Church leaders generally must be open to, and facilitate, a critique of the Church's embodiment of the Christian story. It is imperative that the idealistic criticisms of the young are listened to and respected by the adult Church. Following the example of Pope John Paul II, Church leaders should openly apologize for past mistakes and bad pastoral practice. Most importantly, the ideas and proposals of the rising generation need to be taken seriously in the restructuring of the faith community and in designing the approach to religious education and pastoral ministry. In this way, young people will be given the opportunity to make a significant contribution to the reshaping of the religious culture that they have inherited.

From a Christian perspective, the message and ministry of Jesus is the catalyst for educating in a mutually critical fashion. It is the story of Jesus the Nazarene and the embodiment of that narrative in the structure of the young Church that should guide the shaping of the contemporary Christian community. By educating in a mutually critical fashion, postmodern youth can be fruitfully engaged in a constructive dialogue between their ancient religious tradition and the culture in which they stand. This will require much intentionality on the part of religious educators, youth ministers, university chaplains, and pastors. Yet it is a worthy task if it helps the rising generation to critically embrace the Catholic signifying system as ultimate while it is being embraced by a culture that claims ultimacy for its meaning and values.

Intentional Community Building

From the outset, Christianity has been a communally based religious belief system. It is clear from very early Church life that authentic Christianity belongs to a communal context. 'To reduce Christian faith to personal religious sentiment is to reject the thought and action of the earliest Christian communities'.[20] Among other things, the privatization of life resulting from modernity has produced a non-communal religious faith that is characteristic of many young people today. However, while the atomization of life, now clearly evident in an increasingly urbanized Irish landscape, is a major challenge to the Catholic Church, there are signs among the rising generation of a new search for community. This is illustrated in the interviews and, according to Philip Fogarty, is reflected in the trend of increasing numbers drifting 'to various sects or other groups that give them a feeling of belonging that the Church fails to provide'.[21]

The post-modern sensibility that leads young people to search for a meaningful experience of community is both a challenge and an opportunity for the Catholic Church in contemporary Ireland. A core principle that should guide its pastoral ministry to the young generation is that of intentional community building. There are clear indications, as was illustrated in the interviews, that post-modern youth are involved in a threefold search: the experience of an intimate, non-uniform caring community; the experience of transcendence; and a sense of mission. It is somewhat ironic that this is precisely what the Christian Church has had to offer right from its birth. Presently, young people do not have a sense of belonging to a faith community in which they are provided with an appropriate spirituality and opportunities for relevant action. The lack of involvement and the feeling of being preached at from above produce alienation.

The only kind of community building that will have any attraction for a postmodern generation will be that which is genuinely participative. Otherwise they will not be interested. Michael Warren believes that, for the most part, young people are so long in a 'systematic diminishment of gifts that they figure there is no use in even trying to have a say, and so they just drop out'.[22] Schillebeeckx emphasizes the importance of decision-making participation by all people in the local Church.[23] One certainly agrees with this position, but this is especially important for youth if they are going to remain in many parishes as currently structured. In the process of intentional community building, young people should be given the opportunity to contribute to the development of the religious culture therein.

The best approach to community building, especially in larger parishes, is to begin by developing small subcommunities within the overall community of faith. Each of these may be facilitated by a suitably qualified adult who would meet with them regularly. These meetings should involve discussion, scripture study and reflection, prayer and pastoral action, as well as an occasional celebration of the Eucharist. In order to strengthen the sense of belonging to the total parish community, all of the small groups should come together at regular intervals. Together they should be given responsibility for one of the Sunday Masses, each group taking responsibility for a particular aspect of the liturgy. Furthermore, each small community can have a representative on the parish pastoral council and thereby share ownership of the local *ecclesia*.

The Centrality of the Eucharist

It is clear from the recent quantitative research that has been carried out in Ireland that the Catholic Church is faced with the task of recovering the centrality of the Eucharist. In emphasizing the importance of building community in order to counteract the vague sense of belonging that characterizes the position of many Christians today, Berard Marthaler says that the primary symbol of the ecclesial community is the Eucharistic assembly.[24] In writing about religious socialization, Westerhoff and Kennedy Neville argue that those who have responsibility for the Church's educational ministry should explore afresh the liturgical life as a central element in the life of faith.[25] Gabriel Moran believes that 'The educational formation of a Catholic rests first not on catechetics but on worship and service' and that 'One learns to be a Catholic by participating in the liturgical life of the community.'[26] Michael Drumm claims that 'When Jesus said, 'Do this in memory (*anamnesis*) of me,' he was giving an explicit command to his followers to celebrate his memory through ritual.'[27] It is my conviction that the celebration of the Eucharist is central to discipleship of Jesus the Nazarene. The writings of the early Church make it clear that the first Christians remembered and encountered the risen Lord in a unique way through the ritual of the 'breaking of bread.' This eucharistic ritual was an essential element in its self-understanding and sense of mission.

Since liturgy is the bearer of the Christian story in word and action, there is an urgent need today to breathe new life into the celebration of the Eucharist. One of the principles at the heart of religious education and pastoral ministry among the rising generation should be that of good liturgical catechesis. This is effected as much by the experience of meaningful liturgy as it is by the communication of liturgical knowledge. In school-based religious education, adolescents may be led to explore the nature of ritual, sign and symbol. The interview conversations illustrate that contemporary youth do have a feel for ritual, but they experience the central ritual of the Mass as dead and uninspiring. Two things are necessary in response to this. First, adolescents need to be educated into an appreciation of the rich and ancient symbolism of the Catholic tradition. Second, the way in which the symbols are used needs to be reappraised in order to see if this is appropriate to the cultural experience of a post-modern generation. It is ironic that while young people today appear to have a greater feel for ritual, secular and religious, than the adult generation, they are not drawn to the official ritual of the Church. This may be related to Westerhoff's observation that the change in people's understandings, meanings and way of life, which corresponds with cultural change, results in the growing irrelevance of old rituals that inspired and sustained previous generations. If this is true, it supports the call for an adaptation, a re-energizing, and an appropriate use of the ancient symbols.

Outside of the school-based educational setting, much liturgical work needs to be done with parish and diocesan youth groups, as well as students on college campuses. This should begin with an exploration of the phenomenon of ritual, then focus on young people's experience of contemporary secular ritual, and eventually lead to a discovery of the rich symbolism and ritual that is enmeshed in the Christian narrative. However, all of liturgical education will be incomplete unless young people are exposed to meaningful liturgies that are celebrated in a context that provides an experience of transcendence, intimate community, and unity in diversity. This especially applies to the celebration of the Eucharist.

Since taking part in the eucharistic assembly is determinative of full Christian discipleship, liturgical education that is centred on the Eucharist is indispensable. The word 'transubstantiation', or its equivalent, is no longer part of young people's vocabulary and they generally appear to have lost the strong sense of the unique presence of the risen Lord in the species of bread and wine which was characteristic of previous generations. Nothing has replaced the theology of transubstantiation; thus there is nothing to draw young people to a religious ritual that the majority do not experience as meaningful or relevant. In this regard, it is interesting to note that during the interviews with Fiona she states that, even though she finds the celebration of the Eucharist in most instances frustrating and deadening, she is drawn to attend Mass at fairly frequent intervals. She reported: 'The reason I kind of put up with all that is that I believe that I need the Eucharist; I need Eucharist to keep me going and I need to know that Jesus is there with me, and He tells me that every time he gives me Eucharist.' Fiona was the only one of the five who were interviewed who expressed deep faith in the unique presence of the risen Lord in the eucharistic species of bread and wine.

Church leaders would do well to listen to the voice of one young person who has deep faith in the Eucharistic presence of Christ as she described the kind of Eucharistic celebration that would draw her each weekend. Fiona describes an 'alive' celebration of the Eucharist as follows:

One that is a celebration for a start. This is supposed to be a gift and a gift is supposed to be something that is a happy event . . . and here we are sitting there in pews practically asleep. It should be full of life, and it should be full of the celebration of the life that is in each person, a celebration of each person's gifts and a meeting of those gifts with the gift of Jesus. . . . There is no point in singing a Latin chant if you are a teenager who does not understand Latin, and it is not your music and it is not a celebration for you. It has to be a celebration for each person who is there and it has to be in the language of the people who are there. Otherwise it is irrelevant; it is like a two-way conversation that is going nowhere.

If the Catholic Church is to be successful in restoring the Mass to a central place in the lives of the rising post-modern generation, careful liturgical education and relevant, meaningful celebration are absolutely essential.

Inculturation
Ellis Nelson, Westerhoff, Westerhoff and Kennedy Neville, and Marthaler have each made significant contributions to the concept of religious socialization from their own particular angles. While differing in some respects, their model of religious socialization is based on the concept of socialization that is used by anthropologists and sociologists to describe how a particular culture's beliefs, meanings, values and mores are passed on to each new generation. Ellis Nelson emphasizes how the faith community as a whole can be critically conscious in interpreting the determinative influence of culture on a person's life, as it deliberately communicates the Christian vision of life to children and young people. Westerhoff, Westerhoff and Kennedy Neville, and Marthaler focus on the importance of belonging to a faith community that gives a central place to ritual in the intentional religious socialization process.

The religious socialization model has much to recommend it. It is especially suitable as a comprehensive way of understanding the faith formation of children and younger adolescents. One wonders, however, about its suitability for the religious education of older adolescents in the era of post-modernity. This is particularly true if it is understood in terms of the socializer directly influencing the socializee in a one-way communication process. Apart from the fact that contemporary adolescents and young adults resent their life and religious beliefs being determined by a teacher or other adult, one-way communication is not a good model for either education or religious education. Westerhoff began to recognize the lack of mutual engagement that could be a mark of intentional religious socialization. Only if one accepts Marthaler's understanding of socialization as interaction will the socialization model of religious education be appropriate in the contemporary cultural situation. Young people today want to influence, as well as be influenced by, the religious culture in which they find themselves. Furthermore, a valid use of an interactive socialization model of religious education requires the religious educator to promote growth in personal faith, religious affiliation and the maintenance and transmission of a religious tradition in a thoroughly experiential manner, that is, by integrating the faith story with daily human experience.

A guiding principle that should encompass all of the principles underpinning a post-modern educational and pastoral approach to the challenge facing the Catholic Church in Ireland at the dawn of the third millennium of Christianity is that of inculturation. Peter Schineller believes that all ministry involves the principles and attitudes of inculturation. He points to three key moments in Christian history that intersect with the theme of inculturation: the incarnation of Jesus Christ that is the paradigm of inculturation; the Council of Jerusalem where a decision was made to allow non-Jews become Christians without imposing the law of circumcision; the Second Vatican Council which, while not using the term 'inculturation', advocated a listening, dialogical attitude toward both traditional and modern cultures.[28] Aylward Shorter defines the term 'inculturation' as 'the creative and dynamic relationship between the Christian message and a culture or cultures'.[29] The educational and pastoral principle of inculturation is particularly relevant to the post-modern Western world because it does not demand uniformity; rather, it allows for diverse expressions of the Christian faith within the unity of the one Catholic Church.

Much of what George Albert Coe had to say about the transformation of Christian education is relevant to the theme of inculturation and the culture of post-modernity.[30] He criticized the understanding of religious education that entails passing on an unchanging deposit of faith in a non-dialogical manner. The task of the religious educator is not to impose truth but to promote growth in faith and the free self-expression of the individual. Coe's ideal of transforming the social order into a 'democracy of God' through Christian education is very close to the notion of inculturation. In a similar fashion to Coe, Lane calls for the transformation of both faith and culture in the process of inculturating the gospel message.[31] Thus, while the language of inculturation is new, the idea surfaced many years ago, and may indeed be traced back to the early Church.

During the fifth century, St Patrick and the early Irish missionaries appear to have approached their work of evangelization on the basis of the theological concept of inculturation. Patrick and his fellow missionaries did not condemn the Celtic patterns of belief and practice which they found in this rich and sophisticated culture. Instead, they set out to Christianize them, thereby developing with the people a Christian vision of life that was enriched by the Celtic tradition – a model form of inculturation.

As was pointed out in Chapter III, this unique brand of Catholicism and Christian Celtic spirituality persisted in Ireland until the Famine of 1845. Having survived the onslaught of the Reformation and Counter-Reformation, it was not until after the human and spiritual devastation caused by the Famine that Irish Catholicism was eventually Romanized. As history unfolds, it appears that the losses occasioned by the development outweighed the gains. The institutionalization of the Irish Church led to a decline in popular devotions and in the natural transmission of the faith among the people as a whole. The responsibility for faith formation was increasingly handed over to the institution and to those in authority within it. In a word, a process of inculturation, so characteristic of Irish Christianity, came to an end.

Many of those who have ceased practising the Catholic faith or who have left the Church are turning to Celtic spirituality, either consciously or unconsciously. This is illustrated in the conversations with the five young people who were interviewed. Brigid and Fiona, in particular, have a deep sense of the presence of God in nature and in people. Their spirituality is holistic and they believe in living in harmony with other human beings, the earth, and God. While they may not name their spirituality as Celtic, their spiritual outlook clearly resonates with John O'Donohue's description of Celtic spirituality:

> The Celtic mind was not burdened by dualism, it did not separate what belongs together. The Celtic imagination articulated the inner friendship which embraces nature, divinity, underworld and human world as one. The dualism which separates the visible from the invisible, time from eternity, the human from the divine, was totally alien to them.[32]

For the Celts the world was deeply spiritual. They had a powerful sense of how the visible and the invisible are interconnected. It would have been alien to them to consider spirit in terms of the invisible alone. Nature was regarded as the direct expression of the divine imagination and the most intimate reflection of God's beauty. In one of the oldest Christian Celtic prayers, St Patrick's Breastplate, there is no separation between subjectivity and the elements. Within this worldview, the human face shone as the icon of intimacy. 'It is here,' O'Donohue says, 'in this icon of human presence, that divinity in creation comes nearest to itself'. Nowhere else is there such intimate access to the mystery we name God. Throughout conversation in the native Irish language, there is an explicit recognition that the divine is present in others. One can easily observe the similarity between this theological stance and the basis of Christian morality that is found in the moral section of the Catechism of the Catholic Church, namely, that the human being is made in the image of God.

Catechesi Tradendae states that part of the task of catechesis is to know cultures and their essential components: 'It will learn their most significant expressions; it will respect their particular values and riches.'[33] When applying the theological concept of inculturation to the contemporary Irish cultural scene, it is entirely appropriate to revisit Christian Celtic spirituality. There is an uncanny closeness between this worldview, the recent wave of ecological sensitivity in many parts of the globe, and the human and spiritual sensitivity of a postmodern youth generation. It is my belief that, if the Catholic Church, in its religious education and youth ministry enterprises, does not incorporate the essential elements of Christian Celtic theology and spirituality into its theory and practice, its efforts at inculturating the gospel message will be diminished. Furthermore, there is evidence that some young people are already opting for a pre-Christian form of Celtic religious practice. As the culture of post-modernity continues to react against the dark elements of modernity, especially the philosophy of 'having' over 'being', there will be a corresponding openness to a Christian message that carries a profound respect for the presence of the Divine in the human and non-human world of nature and for the unity of all of life. If one accepts that God's self-revelation has always occurred and continues to occur within the context of human culture, any clear distinction between the sacred and the secular is meaningless. Inculturation is an interactive process, 'a process,' says Andrew McGrady, 'in which each culture is purified by the religious tradition, and the religious tradition itself is purified by the new culture.'[34]

Conclusion

During the dialogue about what most influences the beliefs, values, attitudes, and behaviour of young people today, each of those who took part were asked if, in their experience, there was a connection between care and influence. Four of them used the word 'definitely' in their response and the fifth used the word 'absolutely'. Fiona put it this way:

> When somebody cares for you, the feeling of being accepted or the feeling of being loved, or whatever, is the strongest feeling . . . emotions are stronger than anything else and it is those things you remember, not words that people say. Words are just words which fall on the ground unless they are kind of experienced through life. When they are lived out you do remember them and they do influence you.

It is her experience that when a young person is cared for by an adult, the carer influences her beliefs, values, and attitudes. 'A personal carer,' she says, 'is someone who touches you and challenges you.' Although parents and family members play a key role in the care-influence nexus, the correlation between care and influence is not confined to them. In Sean's case, an uncle (following the death of his father), in Tom's case a nun and a youth leader, and in Fiona's case a priest played key roles in the formation of their value system. Friends and partners, because they care deeply, also have a major influence on young people's imagination of life.

The deep correlation between care and influence is good news to any organization that seeks to influence the lives of young people. In the present context it is both a heartening revelation and a warning call to the Catholic Church in contemporary Ireland as it seeks to offer the rising generation a religious imagination of life, based on the message and ministry of Jesus the Nazarene, in the face of other cultural agencies that are offering alternative visions, meanings, and ways of life. In applying the principles for a religious education and pastoral approach to youth ministry that are offered here, religious educators, youth ministers, pastors and all those in Church leadership roles need to bear in mind that 'words are just words' unless they are accompanied by deep care and concern for the people to whom they are addressed. Moreover, the compassionate stance of those who work with youth must ultimately, as Tom put it, 'allow freedom in the relationship to decide for yourself.'

Finally, there is much good news for parents arising out of the in-depth interviews. Each of the five young people who were interviewed were deeply influenced by their parents' values and outlook on life. Even though the immediate impact of this influence diminished as they progressed through late adolescence, especially in relation to Church affiliation and liturgical participation, the core human and religious values appear to have remained. Moreover, these young people have a strong desire to pass on to their children, albeit selectively, the values that they have received from their parents. Thus, in the midst of all the cultural influences that are affecting the rising generation, parental influence continues to be a major factor. This, in turn, has significant implications for the vast field of adult religious education.

The successful inculturation of the gospel message into the contemporary Irish cultural landscape will require much energy and enthusiasm on behalf of Church leaders, religious educators, and pastoral care agencies. It will require an attitude of openness and a willingness to dialogue with what may appear at times to be an alien cultural environment. Above all, the adult members of the Church must listen to the voices of young people, hear the cry of a postmodern generation, and answer in word and action: 'We will be there for you'.

Notes

1. J. Holland and P. Henriot, *Social Analysis: Linking Faith and Justice* (New York: Orbis Books, 1995), p. 67.
2. John Paul II, *Faith and Reason* (Dublin: Veritas Publications, 1998), p. 4.
3. K. Rahner, *The Shape of the Church to Come* (New York: The Seabury Press, 1974), p. 93.
4. *Ad gentes,* in *Vatican Council II: Conciliar and Post Conciliar Documents,* ed. A. Flannery (Dublin: Dominican Publications, 1981).
5. Rahner, op. cit., p. 100.
6. P. Freire, *Cultural Action for Freedom* (Cambridge, MA: Harvard Educational Review, 1970).
7. E. McDonagh, *Faith in Fragments* (Dublin: Columba Press, 1996), p. 63.
8. C. P. Christ, *Reweaving the World* (San Francisco: Sierra Club Books, 1990), p. 58.
9. T. Berry, *The Dream of the Earth* (San Francisco: Sierra Club Books, 1988), p. 80.
10. J. R. Sachs, *The Christian Vision of Humanity: Basic Christian Anthropology* (Collegeville, MN: Liturgical Press, 1991), p. 43.
11. John Paul II, *Familiaris Consortio* (Boston: Pauline Books & Media, 1981), p. 41.
12. John Paul II, *Faith and Reason* (Dublin: Veritas Publications, 1998), p. 42.
13. E. Bredin, *Disturbing the Peace: The Way of Disciples* (Dublin: Columba Press, 1985), p. 78.
14. J. H. Yoder, *The Politics of Jesus* (Grand Rapids, MI: William B. Eerdmans, 1994).
15. D. Lane, *Foundations for a Social Theology* (New York: Paulist Press, 1984), p. 30.

16. D. Dorr, *Option for the Poor* (New York: Orbis Books, 1983), p. 95.

17. Lane, op. cit., p. 122.

18. J. L. Elias, *Studies in Theology and Education* (Malabar, FL: Robert E. Krieger, 1986).

19. D. Lane, op. cit.

20. M. Drumm, *Passage to Pasch: Revisiting the Catholic Sacraments* (Dublin: Columba Press, 1998), p. 99.

21. P. Fogarty, *Why Don't They Believe Us? Handing on the Faith in a Changing Society* (Dublin: Columba Press, 1993), p. 50.

22. M. Warren, *Youth, Gospel, Liberation* (Dublin: Veritas, 1998), p. 159.

23. E. Schillebeeckx, *The Church: The Human Story of God* (New York: Crossroads, 1990).

24. B. Marthaler, 'Socialisation as a Model for Catechetics', in *Foundations of Religious Education,* ed. P. O'Hare (New York: Paulist Press, 1978), pp. 64–90.

25. J. H. Westerhoff and G. Kennedy Neville, *Generation to Generation* (New York: The Pilgrim Press, 1974).

26. G. Moran, 'Religious Education After Vatican II', in *Open Catholicism,* eds. D. Efraymson & J. Raines (Collegeville, MN: The Liturgical Press, 1997), p. 162.

27. Drumm, op. cit., p. 140.

28. P. Schineller, *A Handbook on Inculturation* (Mahwah, NJ: Paulist Press, 1990).

29. A. Shorter, *Towards a Theology of Inculturation* (New York: Orbis Press, 1988), p. 11.

30. G. A. Coe, *A Social Theory of Religious Education* (New York: Charles Scribner's Sons, 1917).

31. D. Lane, *Religion and Culture in Dialogue* (Dublin: Columba Press, 1993).

32. J. O'Donohue, *Anam Chara: Spiritual Wisdom from the Celtic World* (London: Bantam Press, 1997), p. 16.

33. John Paul II, *Catechesi Tradendae* (Dublin: Veritas Publications, 1979).

34. A. McGrady, 'Inculturation: An Approach to Media Studies Within Religious Education', *Word in Life* 45(2) (1997), pp. 2–11.

BIBLIOGRAPHY

Address to the sixth symposium of the Council of European Episcopal Conferences, 21 October 1985. *Osservatore Romano,* English edition.

Arendt, H. *The Human Condition.* Chicago: University of Chicago Press, 1958.

Aronowitz, S., and H. A. Giroux. *Post-Modern Education: Politics, Culture and Social Criticism.* Minneapolis, MN: University of Minnesota Press, 1991.

Ary, D., L. Jacobs, and A. Razavich. *Introduction to Research in Education.* 3rd ed. New York: Holt, Rinehart and Winston, 1985.

Bailey, M. *History and Conscience: Studies in Honour of Sean O'Riordan CSsR.* Edited by R. Gallagher and B. McConvery. Dublin: Gill and Macmillan, 1989.

Barzun, J., and H. Graff. *The Modern Researcher.* Boston: Houghton Mifflin, 1992.

Baum, G. *Theology and Society.* New York: Paulist Press, 1987.

Beaudoin, T. *Virtual Faith: The Irreverant Spiritual Quest of Generation X.* San Francisco: Jossey-Bass, 1998.

Berry, T. *The Dream of the Earth.* San Francisco: Sierra Club Books, 1988.

Bertaux, D., ed. *Biography and Society: The Life History Approach in the Social Sciences.* Beverly Hills, CA: Sage, 1981.

Boff, L. *Jesus Christ Liberator.* New York: Orbis Books, 1978.

Bogdan, R. C., and S. K. Biklen. *Qualitative Research for Education: An Introduction to Theory and Method.* Boston: Allyn and Bacon, 1992.

Borg, M. J. *Jesus: A New Vision.* San Francisco: Harper, 1991.

Borg, W., and M. Gall. *Educational Research: An Introduction.* 3rd ed. New York: Longman, 1979.

Brause, R., and J. Mayher. *Search and Research: What the Inquiring Teacher Needs to Know.* New York: The Falmer Press, 1994.

Bredin, E. *Disturbing the Peace: The Way of Disciples.* Dublin: Columba Press, 1985.

Breen, R., and C. Whelan. *Social Class and Social Mobility in Ireland.*
Dublin: Gill and Macmillan, 1996.

Brelsford, T. 'Religious Faith and Pluralistic Consciousness'. Paper
presented at the annual meeting of the APRRE Conference,
Orlando, FL, November 1998.

Brennan, O. V. 'Report on Armagh Diocesan "Listening Day"'.
Unpublished report, 1996.

Bronfenbrenner, U. *The Ecology of Human Development: Experiments
by Nature and Design.* Cambridge, MA: Harvard University Press,
1979.

Breslin, A., and J. A. Weaver. Maynooth: Research and Development
Unit of Irish Catholic Church. 1984.

Brown, R. *Responses to 101 Questions on the Bible.* New York: Paulist
Press, 1990.

Carey, J. W. *Communications As Culture.* Boston: Unwin Hyman,
1988.

Cassidy, E. G. *Faith and Culture in the Irish Context.* Dublin: Veritas
Publications, 1996.

Christ, C. P. *Reweaving the World.* San Francisco: Sierra Club Books,
1990.

Coe, G. A. *A Social Theory of Religious Education.* New York: Charles
Scribner's Sons, 1917.

Crowe, F. E. *A Third Collection: Papers by Bernard J. F. Lonergan SJ.*
London: Geoffrey Chapman, 1985.

Dalton, A. 'Befriending an Estranged Home'. *Religious Education* 85,
(1990), 15–24.

Dawson, C. *Religion and Culture.* New York: Meridian Books, 1958.

Dorr, D. *Option for the Poor.* New York: Orbis Books, 1983.

Doyle McCarthy, E. *Knowledge As Culture: The New Sociology of
Knowledge.* London: Routledge, 1996.

Drumm, M. 'A People Formed by Ritual'. *Faith and Culture in the
Irish Context.* Edited by E. G. Cassidy. Dublin: Veritas
Publications, 1996.

Drumm, M. *Passage to Pasch: Revisiting the Catholic Sacraments.*
Dublin: The Columba Press, 1998.

Dunne, J. S. *The Way of All the Earth.* Notre Dame: University of
Notre Dame Press, 1978.

Dunne, J. 'Religion and Modernity: Reading the Signs'. *Faith and Culture in the Irish Context.* Edited by E. G. Cassidy. Dublin: Veritas Publications, 1996.

Egan, J. *The Death of Metaphor.* Newbridge, Ireland: The Kavanagh Press, 1990.

Egan, K. *The Educated Mind: How Cognitive Tools Shape Our Understanding.* Chicago: University of Chicago Press, 1997.

Elias, J. L. *Studies in Theology and Education.* Malabar, FL: Robert E. Krieger, 1986.

Elias, J. L. *Religion, Society and Culture.* (1999) Unpublished manuscript.

Elias, J. L. and S. Merriam. *Philosophical Foundations of Adult Education.* Malabar, FL: Robert E. Krieger, 1980.

Ellis Nelson, C. *Where Faith Begins.* Atlanta, GA: John Knox Press, 1971.

Feeney, J. 'Can a World View Be Healed? Students and Postmodernism'. *America* 177 (1997), 12–16.

Flannery, T. *From the Inside: A Priest's View of the Catholic Church.* Cork: Mercier Press, 1999.

Fogarty, P. *Why Don't They Believe Us? Handing on the Faith in a Changing Society.* Dublin: Columba Press, 1993.

Foucault, M. *The Foucauld Reader.* New York: Pantheon Books, 1984.

Freire, P. *Cultural Action for Freedom.* Cambridge, MA: Harvard Educational Review, 1970.

Freyne, S. *The World of the New Testament.* Wilmington, DE: Michael Glazier, 1980.

Gallagher, M. P. *Clashing Symbols: An Introduction to Faith and Culture.* London: Darton, Longman, & Todd, 1997.

Geertz, C. *The Interpretations of Cultures.* New York: Basic Books, 1973.

Gergen, K. *The Saturated Self: Dilemmas of Identity in Contemporary Life.* New York: Basic Books, 1991.

Gill, J. *Learning to Learn: Toward a Philosophy of Education.* Atlantic Highlands, NJ: Humanities Press International, 1993.

Greeley, A. *Religion: A Secular Theory.* New York: Transaction, 1982.

Greeley, A. *Religion and Poetry.* New York: Transaction, 1995.

Griffin, D. R. Introduction to *Varieties of Postmodern Theory.* Edited by D. R. Griffin, W. A. Beardslee, and J. Holland. Albany, NY: State University of New York, 1989.

Groome, T. H. *Christian Religious Education: Sharing Our Story and Vision.* San Francisco: Harper and Row, 1980.

Groome, T. H. *Sharing Faith: A Comprehensive Approach to Religious Education and Pastoral Ministry: The Way of Shared Praxis.* San Francisco: Harper and Row, 1991.

Groome, T. H. 'Post-Modernism: The Challenges and Opportunities for Religious Education.' Paper presented at the annual meeting of the APRRE Conference, Orlando, FL, November 1998.

Gula, R. M. *Reason Informed by Faith: Foundations of Catholic Morality.* New York: Paulist Press, 1989.

Gutierrez, G. *A Theology of Liberation.* New York: Orbis Books, 1973.

Gutierrez, G. *We Drink From Our Own Wells.* New York: Orbis Books, 1983.

Hanley, A. 'Attitudes to the Catholic Church: The RTÉ Prime Time/MRBI Survey.' Maynooth, Ireland: Council for Research and Development, 1998.

Hanley, A. 'Major Religious Confidence Survey.' *Intercom,* March 1998, pp. 18–19.

Harvey, V. A. *The Historian and the Believer: The Morality of Historical Knowledge and Christian Belief.* New York: Macmillan, 1996.

Hess, M. E. 'From trucks carrying messages to ritualized identities: Implications of the postmodern paradigm shift in media studies for religious education.' Paper presented at the annual meeting of the APRRE Conference, Orlando, FL, November, 1998.

Hessel, D. T. *Social Ministry.* Louisville, KY: Westminster/John Knox Press, 1992.

Holland, J. and P. Henriot. *Social Analysis: Linking Faith and Justice.* New York: Orbis Books, 1995.

Horan, M. 'Making Connections: Ministry to Youth and Young Adults in Postmodern Culture.' Paper presented at the annual meeting of the APRRE Conference, Orlando, FL, November 1998.

Horell, H. 'Fostering Critical Reflection in a Postmodern Milieu.'

Paper presented at the annual meeting of the APRRE Conference, Orlando, FL, November 1998.

Hyland, M. *Children of God Series.* Dublin: Veritas Publications, 1987.

Inglehart, R. *Culture Shift in Advanced Industrial Society.* Princeton: Princeton University Press, 1990.

John Paul II, Pope. *Catechesi tradendae.* Dublin: Veritas Publications, 1979.

John Paul II, Pope. *Familiaris consortio.* Boston: Pauline Books and Media, 1981.

John Paul II, Pope. *Christifideles Laici.* Dublin: Veritas Publications, 1988.

John Paul II, Pope. *Faith and Reason.* Dublin: Veritas Publications, 1998.

John Paul II, Pope. *The Ecological Crisis: A Common Responsibility.* Washington, DC: United States Catholic Conference, 1989.

John Paul II, Pope. *Centesimus annus.* Dublin: Veritas Publications, 1991.

Johnson-Siebold, J. 'Simultaneous Religious Education: Preschool and Postmodern.' Paper presented at the annual meeting of the APRRE Conference, Orlando, FL, November, 1998.

Kaplan, A. *The Conduct of Inquiry: Methodology for Behavioral Science.* New Brunswick, NJ: Transaction, 1998.

Kavanaugh, J. F. *Following Christ in a Consumer Society.* New York: Orbis Books, 1991.

Kegan, R. *In Over Our Heads: The Mental Demands of Modern Life.* Cambridge, MA: Harvard University Press, 1994.

Kellner, D. *Media Culture.* London: Routledge, 1995.

Kristeva, J. *Strangers to Ourselves.* New York: Columbia University Press, 1989.

Kroeber, A. L., and D. Kluckhohn. *Culture: A Critical Review of Concepts and Definitions.* New York: Vintage Books, 1963.

Lamoureux, P. A. 'Emotion, Imagination and the Role of the Spirit', *New Theology Review* 11 (1998), 57–62.

Lane, D. *Foundations for a Social Theology.* New York: Paulist Press, 1984.

Lane, D. *Religion and Culture in Dialogue.* Dublin: Columba Press, 1993.

Larkin, E. *The Historical Dimensions of Irish Catholicism.* Washington, DC: Catholic University of America Press, 1984.

Legg, P. M. 'Contemporary Films and Religious Exploration: An Opportunity for Religious Education', *Religious Education* 92 (1997), 120–136.

Leuze, T. 'Is Shared Christian Praxis Postmodern? An Anglo-American Postmodern Consideration.' Paper presented at the annual meeting of the APRRE Conference, Orlando, FL, November 1998.

Levi-Strauss, C. *Student Anthropology.* Vol. 1. New York: Basic Books, 1963.

Lincoln, Y. S. and E. G. Giba. *Naturalistic Inquiry.* Beverly Hills, CA: Sage, 1985.

Linton, R. *The Cultural Background of Personality.* New York: D. Appleton-Century, 1945.

Lonergan, B. *Insight: A Study of Human Understanding.* London: Longman, Green, 1958.

Lonergan, B. *Method in Theology.* London: Darton, Longman, and Todd, 1972.

Lonergan, B. *A Second Collection.* Edited by W. F. J. Ryan and B. J. Tyrrell. Philadelphia: The Westminster Press, 1974.

Long, J. *Generating Hope: A Strategy for Reaching the Postmodern Generation.* Downers Grove, IL: Intervarsity Press, 1997.

Lubac, H. de. *The Christian Resistance to Anti-Semitism: Memories from 1940–1944.* San Francisco: Ignatius Press, 1990.

Ludwig, R. A. *Reconstructing Catholicism: For a New Generation.* New York: Crossroad, 1995.

Lynn, R. W., and E. Wright. *The Big Little School.* New York: Harper and Row, 1971.

Lyons, E., *Jesus: Self-Portrait by God.* Dublin: Columba Press, 1994.

MacGreil, M. *Prejudice in Ireland Revisited.* Maynooth: Survey and Research Unit, 1996.

Marthaler, B. 'Socialization as a Model for Catechetics.' In *Foundations of Religious Education.* Edited by P. O'Hare. New York: Paulist Press, 1978.

McCormack, B. *Perceptions of Saint Patrick in Eighteenth-Century Ireland.* Dublin: Fourt Courts Press, 2000.

McCracken, G. *The Long Interview*. Newbury Park, CA: Sage, 1988.

McDonagh, E. *Faith in Fragments*. Dublin: Columba Press, 1996.

McGrady, A. 'Inculturation: An Approach to Media Studies Within Religious Education.' *Word in Life* 45 (2) (1997), 2–11.

Metz, J. B. *Faith in History and Society*. London: Burns and Oates, 1980.

Metz, J. B. *The Emergent Church: The Future of Christianity in a Postbourgeois World*. Translated by P. Mann. New York: Crossroads, 1981.

Mishler, E. G. *Research Interviewing*. Cambridge, MA: Harvard University Press, 1986.

Moran, G. 'Religious Education After Vatican II'. In *Open Catholicism*. Edited by D. Efroymson and J. Raines. Collegeville, MN: The Liturgical Press, 1997.

Murphy, N. *Theology in the Age of Scientific Reasoning*. Ithaca, NY: Cornell University Press, 1990.

Murphy, N. *Anglo-American Postmodernity: Philosophical Perspectives on Science, Religion, and Ethics*. Boulder, CO: Westview Press, 1997.

Murphy, N., and J. W. McClendon. 'Distinguishing Modern and Postmodern Theologies.' *Modern Theology* 5 (1989), 192–210.

Murray, D. 'Faith and Culture: A Complex Relationship'. In *Faith and Culture in the Irish Context*. Edited by E. G. Cassidy. Dublin: Veritas Publications, 1996.

Newman, J. H. *Grammar of Assent*. London: Longman, 1901.

Nic Ghiolla Phadraig, A. 'Survey on Belief and Practice Among Irish Catholics.' Dublin: Research and Development Unit of the Irish Catholic Church, 1974.

Nichols, K. *Refracting the Light: Learning the Languages of Faith*. Dublin: Veritas Publications, 1997.

Niebuhr, H. R. *Christ and Culture*. New York: Harper and Row, 1951.

Niebuhr, H. R. *Radical Monotheism and Western Culture*. New York: Harper and Row, 1970.

Nye, R. B. *This Almost Chosen People*. Ann Arbor, MI: Michigan State University Press, 1966.

O'Brien, M. 'Practical Theology and Postmodern Religious

Education.' Paper presented at the annual meeting of the APRRE Conference, Orlando, FL, November 1998.

O'Donohue, J. *Anam Chara: Spiritual Wisdom from the Celtic World.* London: Bantam Press, 1997.

O'Gorman, R. 'Towards a Postmodern Model of Spirituality for Congregational Studies.' Paper presented at the annual meeting of the APRRE Conference, Orlando, FL, November 1998.

O'Murchu, D. *Reclaiming Spirituality: A New Spiritual Framework for Today's World.* Dublin: Gill and Macmillan, 1997.

O'Riordain, J. J. *Irish Catholics: Tradition and Transition.* Dublin: Veritas Publications, 1980.

Pastoral Constitution on the Church in the Modern World: *Gaudium et spes. Vatican Council II: The Conciliar and Post Conciliar Documents.* Edited by A. Flannery. Dublin: Dominican Publications, 1981.

Patrick, A. E. 'Imaginative Literature and the Renewal of Moral Theology'. *New Theology Review* 11 (1998), 43–56.

Patton, M. Q. *How to Use Qualitative Methods in Evaluation.* Newbury Park, CA: Sage, 1987.

Phenix, P. *Realms of Meaning.* New York: McGraw-Hill, 1964.

Rahner, K. *The Shape of the Church to Come.* New York: The Seabury Press, 1974.

Reed, S., ed. *Spirituality.* New Rochelle, NY: Don Bosco MultiMedia, 1991.

'Religious Confidence Survey.' *The Irish Times.* 4 February 1998.

Roebben, B. 'The Vulnerability of the Postmodern Educator: Towards a New Encounter Between Theology and Education.' Paper presented at the annual meeting of the APRRE Conference, Orlando, FL, November 1998.

Rorty, R. 'Solidarity of Objectivity.' In *Post Analytic Philosophy.* Edited by H. Rachman and C. West. New York: Columbia University Press, 1985.

Rouner, L. S., ed. *Civil Religion and Political Theology.* Notre Dame, IN: Notre Dame Press, 1986.

Sachs, J. R. *The Christian Vision of Humanity: Basic Christian Anthropology.* Collegeville, MN: Liturgical Press, 1991.

Schillebeeckx, E. *The Church: The Human Story of God.* New York: Crossroads, 1990.

Schineller, P. *A Handbook on Inculturation*. Mahwah, NJ: Paulist Press, 1990.

Schuman, D. *Policy Analysis, Education, and Everyday Life*. Lexington, MA: Heath, 1982.

Schutz, A. *The Phenomenology of the Social World*. Translated by G. Walsh and F. Lenhert. Chicago: Northwestern University Press, 1967.

Seidman, I. E. *Interviewing as Qualitative Research: A Guide for Researchers in Education and the Social Sciences*. New York: Teachers College Press, 1991.

Shelton Smith, H. *Faith and Nurture*. New York: Scribner, 1941.

Shorter, A. *Towards a Theology of Inculturation*. New York: Orbis Press, 1988.

Sorri, M. and J. Gill. *A Postmodern Epistemology: Language, Truth and Body*. Lewiston, NY: Edwin Mellen Press, 1989.

Swidler, A. 'Culture in Action: Symbols and Strategies.' *American Sociological Review* 51 (April 1986), 273–286.

Taylor, C. *The Ethics of Authenticity*. Cambridge, MA: Harvard University Press, 1991.

Tracy, D. *Blessed Rage for Order: The New Pluralism in Theology*. New York: Seabury Press, 1975.

Tracy, D. 'Theology and the Many Faces of Postmodernity.' *Theology Today* 51 (1994), 104–114.

Tylor, E. B. *Primitive Culture*. Vol. 1. London: John Murray, 1871.

US Catholic Bishops. *To Teach As Jesus Did*. Washington, DC: Author, 1973.

Vygotsky, L. *Mind in Society: The Development of Higher Psychological Processes*. Cambridge, MA: Harvard University Press, 1978.

Vygotsky, L. *Thought and Language*. Cambridge, MA: MIT Press, 1986.

Warren, M. *Communications and Cultural Analysis*. Westport, CT: Bergin and Garvey, 1992.

Warren, M. *Youth, Gospel, Liberation*. Dublin: Veritas Publications, 1998.

Westerhoff, J. H. *Will Our Children Have Faith?* New York: The Seabury Press, 1976.

Westerhoff, J. H., and G. Kennedy Neville. *Generation to Generation*. New York: The Pilgrim Press, 1974.

Whelan, C. T. and T. Fahey. 'Religious change in Ireland 1981–1990.' In *Faith and Culture in the Irish Context.* Edited by E. G. Cassidy. Dublin: Veritas Publications, 1996.

Whelan, C. T., D. Hannon and S. Creighton. 'Unemployment, Poverty and Psychological Distress.' *Journal of Social Policy* 22 (1991), 141–172.

Whelan, W. 'Postmodernism in the Work of Julia Kristeva.' Paper presented at the annual meeting of the APRRE Conference, Orlando, FL, November 1998.

Williams, R. *The Sociology of Culture.* New York: Schocken Books, 1981.

Yankelovich, D. *The New Morality: A Profile of American Youth in the 1970s.* New York: McGraw-Hill, 1974.

Yoder, J. H. *The Politics of Jesus.* Grand Rapids, MI: William B. Eerdmans, 1994.